CAMPAIGN 279

APPOMATTOX 1865

Lee's last campaign

RON FIELD

ILLUSTRATED BY ADAM HOOK
Series editor Marcus Cowper

First published in Great Britain in 2015 by Osprey Publishing,
PO Box 883, Oxford, OX1 9PL, UK
PO Box 3985, New York, NY 10185-3985, USA
E-mail: info@ospreypublishing.com

A CIP catalog record for this book is available from the British Library.

ISBN: 978 1 4728 0751 9
PDF e-book ISBN: 978 1 4728 0752 6
e-Pub ISBN: 978 1 4728 0753 3

Editorial by Ilios Publishing Ltd, Oxford, UK (www.iliospublishing.com)
Index by Alison Worthington
Typeset in Myriad Pro and Sabon
Maps by Bounford.com
3D bird's-eye views by The Black Spot
Battlescene illustrations by Adam Hook
Originated by PDQ Media, Bungay, UK
Printed in China through Worldprint Ltd.

15 16 17 18 19   10 9 8 7 6 5 4 3 2 1

ARTIST'S NOTE

Readers may care to note that the original paintings from which the color
plates in this book were prepared are available for private sale. The
Publishers retain all reproduction copyright whatsoever. The artist can be
contacted at the following address:
Scorpio, 158 Mill Road, Hailsham, East Sussex BN27 2SH, UK
Email: scorpiopaintings@btinternet.com
The Publishers regret that they can enter into no correspondence upon this
matter.

THE WOODLAND TRUST

Osprey Publishing are supporting the Woodland Trust, the UK's leading
woodland conservation charity, by funding the dedication of trees.

ACKNOWLEDGEMENTS

The author would like to thank the following for their help and support:
Patrick Shroeder, Historian, Appomattox Court House National Historical
Park; Chris M. Calkins, Park Manager, Sailor's Creek Battlefield Historical
State Park; Marlana L. Cook, Curator of Art, West Point Museum; Paul R.
Ackermann, Museum Specialist/Conservator, West Point Museum; Michael
J. McAfee, Curator of History, West Point Museum; Michael C. Lucas,
Historian, High Bridge Battlefield Museum; Peter Harrington, Curator, Anne
S. K. Brown Military Collection, Providence, Rhode Island; Christopher
Morton, Assistant Curator, New York State Military Museum; Bob Bradley,
Curator of Military History, Alabama Department of Archives and History;
Meredith McDonough, Archivist, Alabama Department of Archives and
History; Ashley L. Wolff, Museum Registrar, Collections Management,
Pennsylvania Historical and Museum Commission; Bruce Bazelon,
Pennsylvania Historical and Museum Commission; Jamison Davis, Visual
Resources Manager, Virginia Historical Society; Cindy Harriman, Executive
Director, Texas Civil War Museum; Greg Mast, Jay Barringer, Kenneth W.
Miller, Bill Elswick and Matthew Wallace-Gross.

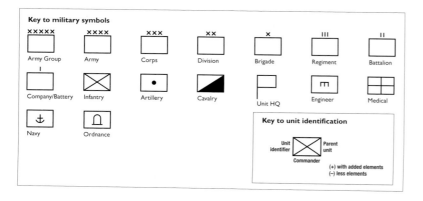

CONTENTS

ORIGINS OF THE CAMPAIGN   5

CHRONOLOGY   8

OPPOSING COMMANDERS   9
Confederate ▪ Union

OPPOSING FORCES   13
Confederate ▪ Union ▪ Order of battle

OPPOSING PLANS   22

THE CAMPAIGN   24
The fall of Petersburg and Richmond, March 29–April 3 ▪ Confederate withdrawal from Petersburg
and Richmond, April 2–3 ▪ Union occupation and pursuit, April 3

AFTERMATH   89

THE BATTLEFIELD TODAY   92

SELECT BIBLIOGRAPHY   94

INDEX   95

Overview of the Appomattox Campaign, March 25–April 9, 1865.

1. March 25. To reduce the threat of a Union attack on the right flank of the Petersburg line, Gordon's Corps attacks Fort Stedman. It fails; the Confederate losses of men in killed, wounded and captured has the opposite effect, and weakens his defenses.

2. March 31. After meeting with Lincoln and Sherman at City Point, Virginia, Grant begins the Union spring offensive by marching Sheridan's cavalry plus II and V Corps, Army of the Potomac, towards Dinwiddie Court House to turn Lee's right flank. W.H.F. Lee's cavalry and Pickett's infantry division advance to meet Sheridan's troops and halt them. The Union V Corps attacks the White Oak Road trenches to the northeast. Pickett is forced to withdraw and entrench at Five Forks. Lee orders him to hold this position at all cost.

3. March 31. Warren's V Corps attacks the White Oak Road trenches hoping to cut communications with Pickett at Five Forks. The Union advance is stopped by a counterattack directed by Robert E. Lee himself, but the retreat is halted by Griffin's division. The Confederates fall back with their right flank turned at an angle, and the direct link with Pickett's troops at Five Forks is severed.

4. April 1. While Sheridan's cavalry pins down Pickett's troops along the White Oak Road, V Corps assaults the Confederate left flank and rear, winning a decisive victory at Five Forks; it proves to be a breaking point for the Army of Northern Virginia. Attending a shad bake, Pickett is unaware of the battle until it is too late. Though V Corps has performed well, Sheridan relieves Warren of command. Lee orders Field's Division, Longstreet's Corps, south of the James River to bolster his right.

5. April 1–2. Worried that Lee might evacuate the Petersburg trenches during the night and attack Sheridan before support troops can arrive,

Grant orders a bombardment along the entire Petersburg line at 9 p.m. on April 1, following which a mass assault begins at 4.30 a.m. on April 2. Wright's VI Corps breaks through the Confederate trenches along the Boydton Plank Road cutting Lee's army in two. The Confederates fall back to forts Gregg and Whitworth, permitting Lee to evacuate the remains of his army from the Petersburg and Richmond defenses under cover of darkness. The march towards Amelia Court House begins.

6. April 2. Miles's division of Humphreys's II Corps strikes north from the White Oak Road and captures the Southside Railroad at Sutherland's Station, severing Lee's last supply line into Petersburg.

7. April 3. Attempting to escape to Amelia Court House, Confederate forces south of the Appomattox are attacked by Custer's division. Making a stand at Namozine Creek, they withdraw to Namozine Church and Wintercomac Creek where many are captured. However, they buy time for "Rooney" Lee and Bushrod Johnson to find an alternative escape route after discovering that the bridge over Deep Creek is impassable.

8. April 4. Lee's plan to rendezvous at Amelia Court House is hampered by the failure to place a pontoon bridge next to the Genito Bridge, forcing the Confederates to converge on Goode's Bridge. This enables Grant's forces to reach Jetersville and Burkeville and block their path.

9. April 5. Lee is forced to divert his army west via Deatonsville towards Farmville and the Union pursuit continues. Crook's cavalry attacks the main Confederate wagon train from Richmond near Paineville.

10. April 6. A small Union force under Brigadier-General Theodore Read is sent from Burkeville to destroy High Bridge to prevent Lee's army from crossing the Appomattox River. They clash with Lee's cavalry and are

defeated. This action deceives Lee into thinking there is a large Union force ahead of him and he entrenches at Rice's Depot, which delays his progress and enables Grant to gain further ground.

11. April 6. Crook's cavalry blocks the road west of Little Sailor's Creek forcing Ewell to make a stand near the Hillsman farmhouse. Anderson is attacked by the rest of Merritt's cavalry west of the creek at Marshall's Crossroads. The diverted Confederate wagon train protected by Gordon's troops is attacked near Lockett farm. All three Confederate armies are overwhelmed and defeated.

12. April 7. The advancing Union II Corps encounters Confederate forces entrenched on high ground near Cumberland Church covering the escape of their wagon train. They attack twice but are repulsed; nightfall halts the action. Lee's troops silently slip away again under cover of darkness.

13. April 8. Custer's cavalry captures three Confederate supply trains at Appomattox Station loaded with provisions for Lee's army. They then attack Walker's artillery encampment, driving off the Confederate defenders.

14. April 9. Arriving north of Appomattox Court House, Lee orders Gordon and Fitzhugh Lee to attack Sheridan's cavalry blocking his route west, but determines to surrender if infantry is encountered. The Union infantry marches over 30 miles (50km) and arrives in time to support the cavalry. The II and VI Corps close in on the Confederates at New Hope Church and Lee surrenders the Army of Northern Virginia.

0   10 miles

0   10km

N

ORIGINS OF THE CAMPAIGN

The arrival in Washington DC of General Ulysses S. Grant in March 1864 heralded the beginning of the end for the Army of Northern Virginia and would lead to the ultimate defeat of the Confederate States of America. It took over a year from the time Grant assumed responsibility as commander of all Union forces for the final objective to be achieved during which the Overland and Petersburg campaigns were fought by a people exhausted by the Civil War. Along the way thousands more Northern and Southern lives would be lost but by the end of March 1865, about 58,400 Confederate soldiers faced more than 112,000 Union troops of the Army of the Potomac and Army of the James across the siege lines surrounding Petersburg and Richmond. These odds would continue to tilt in favor of the Union with the arrival south of the James River of Major-General Philip H. Sheridan's Union Army of the Shenandoah, which increased the size of the Northern army in Virginia to approximately 120,000 men.

City Point served as Grant's operational base during the siege of Petersburg and the Appomattox Campaign. The supply depot consisted of more than 1.5 miles (2.4km) of wharves and scores of warehouses. A railroad terminal with 25 engines and 275 boxcars, plus thousands of mule-drawn wagons, delivered 1,500 tons of supplies daily to the Union army. (Library of Congress LC-DIG-ppmsca-33290)

From February 1865 two further Union commands moved north through the Carolinas. That of Major-General William T. Sherman had completed its "March to the Sea" from Atlanta to Savannah, Georgia, by December 21, 1864, effectively cutting the Confederacy in two, and by late January 1865 had begun its advance through South Carolina towards Virginia. The other, under Major-General John M. Schofield, had been transported by rail and sea from Tennessee to Fort Fisher, North Carolina, and occupied Wilmington on February 22, 1865, following which it joined forces with Sherman at Goldsboro on March 23, 1865.

The only Confederate force which might prevent a link-up between the forces of Grant and Sherman was the war-weary Army of the Tennessee,

commanded by Lieutenant-General Joseph Johnston, located in central North Carolina. Lee understood that a connection of these Union armies would spell disaster for the South. He was also aware that even if Sherman did not arrive in Virginia, Grant's forces could continue to exert pressure against the Petersburg-Richmond area, thereby strangling his supply lines and starving his army plus the civilian population of both cities. Furthermore, the Confederate commanding general had no prospect of disrupting the vast Union supply system as ships continued to ply up the James River to unload their cargoes of ammunition, weapons and food at City Point about 8 miles (13km) northeast of Petersburg.

On February 8, 1865, Lee wrote to the Confederate Secretary of War John C. Breckinridge alerting him to the dangers inherent in the strategic situation, and advising, "You must not be surprised if calamity befalls us." By this time he realized that his best chance of continuing the war effort and saving what remained of the Confederacy was to somehow extricate the Army of Northern Virginia from behind the siege lines and attempt to link up with Johnston in North Carolina. He spent the next six weeks or so pondering how to undertake this risky maneuver. Meanwhile, incessant rain, muddy roads and the poor condition of the horses forced him to maintain his troops in the trenches defending Petersburg and Richmond.

Meeting aboard the dispatch steamer *River Queen* anchored in the James River on March 27–28, 1865, President Abraham Lincoln, Major-General William T. Sherman, Lieutenant-General Ulysses S. Grant, and Rear Admiral David D. Porter discussed the peace terms to be offered to the Confederates once the Civil War was over. Entitled "The Peace Makers," this painting by G. P. A. Healy depicts the President listening intently to advice from his generals. (Library of Congress LC-USZ62-67405)

At the same time, Grant understood that the survival of Richmond depended on Petersburg, and realized that the latter's position as a manufacturing and transportation center provided supplies that sustained the Confederate capital. In short, if Petersburg fell, Richmond would fall also. The Union commanding general was also aware that Lee might attempt to slip away with his army to join that of Johnston. In his *Personal Memoirs* published in 1895, he wrote: "One of the most anxious periods of my experience during the rebellion was the last few weeks before Petersburg. I felt that the situation of the Confederate army was such that they would try to make an escape at the earliest possible moment, and I was afraid, every morning, that I would awake from my sleep to hear that Lee had gone, and that nothing was left but a picket-line." By March 1865, Grant was convinced that Lee was about to send everything except what was necessary for the immediate defense of Petersburg south by way of the Richmond & Danville Railroad. He knew that Lee's army could move more lightly and rapidly than his own, and if the Confederates got a head start they would leave his ponderous armies behind. As a result, he would have to fight the same opponent farther south, and the war might be prolonged for a further year.

However, Grant was dependent on several factors before he could finally launch his vital spring offensive. Firstly, the winter had been one of sub-zero temperatures, sleet, snow and heavy rain, and the Virginia roads had become impassable for artillery and cavalry. An editorial comment in the *Daily Dispatch* of Richmond concluded on January 24, 1865 that there was "too much mud between the two armies to make a serious advance." Four days later the same newspaper commented: "The troops of the two armies have as much as they can do to keep from freezing. Field operations are out of the question." Secondly, Grant was insistent that Sheridan must join him south of the James River in order that he might maximize his chances of final victory. He needed the extra mobility of Sheridan's two divisions of cavalry to sustain his campaign. After marching and fighting his way into central Virginia from the Shenandoah Valley, Sheridan finally reached City Point on March 26. During the next two days Grant met with President Abraham Lincoln, Major-General Sherman (who had coincidentally decided to take a special trip from North Carolina), and Rear Admiral David D. Porter, aboard the dispatch steamer *River Queen*, to discuss the nature of the peace terms to be offered once the Confederates had finally been defeated. After a further two weeks of fighting which led both armies to Appomattox Court House, the war in Virginia was over.

CHRONOLOGY

1865

March 27	A Union council of war is held at City Point, Virginia.
March 29	The Union assault on Petersburg begins.
March 31	The battles of Dinwiddie Court House and White Oak Road take place.
April 1	Sheridan is victorious at the Battle of Five Forks, southwest of Petersburg, Virginia.
April 2	Battle of Sutherland's Station; Miles's Union division routs Heth's Confederates. Fighting takes place at forts Gregg and Whitworth. The Confederate evacuation of Petersburg and Richmond begins.
April 3	Battles at Namozine Church and Wintercomac Creek.
April 4–5	Confederate rendezvous takes place at Amelia Court House.
April 5	Confederate forces continue to flee westwards; fighting at Jetersville and Painesville.
April 6	The High Bridge Expedition prevents the vital bridge from being fired by Confederate forces. The Battles of Little Sailor's Creek see thousands of Confederate troops captured, including several generals.
April 7	Fighting at Cumberland Church; Confederate forces hold back the Union II Corps.
April 8	The Battle of Appomattox Station; Custer's cavalry captures and destroys the Confederate supply train.
April 9	Following a final engagement, the surrender of Lee's Army of Northern Virginia takes place at Appomattox Court House.

OPPOSITE
Taken in 1864, this is the only known wartime photo of Robert E. Lee in which he wears his military sash and dress sword. By February 1865, Lee was convinced that the only possibility of continuing the war effort and saving the Confederacy was to withdraw the Army of Northern Virginia from the siege lines around Petersburg and Richmond and attempt to join the Army of the Tennessee under Joseph E. Johnston in North Carolina. (Library of Congress LC-DIG-ppmsca-35446)

OPPOSING COMMANDERS

CONFEDERATE

Following his home state out of the Union on April 17, 1861, **Robert E. Lee** rejected an offer from President Abraham Lincoln to command the Union army. Resigning his colonelcy in the 1st Cavalry, he accepted a commission as major-general of Virginia State Forces and served as senior military advisor to CSA President Jefferson Davis. His first Confederate field responsibility came in June 1862 when he led Confederate forces in the Eastern Theater, which he renamed the Army of Northern Virginia. While he achieved victories at the Seven Days Battles, Second Bull Run, Fredericksburg and Chancellorsville, both his attempts to invade the North had limited results. Barely escaping defeat at Sharpsburg (Antietam), in September 1862, he was decisively beaten during the third day at Gettysburg in July 1863. When Grant commenced the Overland Campaign on May 4, 1864, the Army of Northern Virginia inflicted heavy casualties on the larger Union forces, particularly at Cold Harbor, although Lee was unable to replace his own heavy losses. Taking control of the Petersburg defenses in June 1864, he was promoted to general-in-chief of all Confederate forces on January 31, 1865.

Nicknamed "Pete" and known as Lee's "Old War Horse," **James Longstreet** resigned from the United States army in 1861 and was promoted to major-general in the Confederate army, following which he led a division at Yorktown and Williamsburg. Winning Lee's confidence during the Seven Days Battles in 1862, he was given command of I Corps, Army of Northern Virginia. He performed with distinction at Fredericksburg and disagreed with Lee's decision to mount a frontal attack at Gettysburg on July 3, 1863. Sent west to support General Braxton Bragg later that year, he fought at Chickamauga and during the Knoxville Campaign. Rejoining Lee in Virginia for the Wilderness Campaign, he was seriously wounded by friendly fire on May 6, 1864, and was out of action for

over five months. Returning to active service in October, he commanded the Richmond defenses, including all forces north of the James River plus Pickett's Division at Bermuda Hundred, until summoned south of the James on April 2, 1865.

Beginning the war as a major in the 6th Alabama Infantry, **John B. Gordon** received the colonelcy of that regiment on April 28, 1862. He succeeded the wounded General Robert E. Rodes in command of the 1st Brigade, Hill's Division of Thomas J. Jackson's command, Army of Northern Virginia, during the Peninsula Campaign, and was wounded at Sharpsburg on September 17, 1862. He continued to command his brigade of Georgians at Chancellorsville, Gettysburg, the Wilderness and Spotsylvania, and was appointed major-general on May 14, 1864, being given command of II Corps, Army of Northern Virginia.

Becoming colonel of the 13th Virginia Infantry in 1861, **Ambrose P. Hill** was quickly promoted to brigadier-general and by May 1862 had been appointed major-general in command of the "Light Division," so-called because of its speedy marching. He succeeded Jackson after his death at

Chancellorsville and in May 1863 was named a lieutenant-general leading the newly created III Corps which he commanded during the Gettysburg Campaign. During the fall of the same year, Hill failed to conduct sufficient reconnaissance and his infantry was repulsed by Major-General Gouverneur K. Warren's II Corps at Bristoe Station. Intermittently ill during the Overland and Petersburg campaigns, his troops performed well at Cold Harbor and the Battle of the Crater. Suffering from ill-health again during March 1865, he returned to his post on April 1 of that year.

The nephew of Robert E. Lee, **Fitzhugh Lee** (not to be confused with his cousin William Henry Fitzhugh Lee, Robert's second son) served as a staff officer under Joseph E. Johnston after becoming lieutenant-colonel in the 1st Virginia Cavalry in 1861. Appointed a brigadier-general after taking part in the ride around George B. McClellan in 1862, his brigade fought at Antietam, Kelly's Ford and Gettysburg. He became a major-general in August 1863 and led a division at Spotsylvania before joining Jubal Early in the Shenandoah Valley where he was seriously wounded during the Third Battle of Winchester (or Opequon) in 1864. Returning to lead the cavalry north of the James River in January 1865, he replaced Lieutenant-General Wade Hampton as senior cavalry commander of the Army of Northern Virginia on April 2, 1865.

UNION

At the outbreak of Civil War, **Ulysses S. Grant** offered his services to Illinois Governor Richard Yates and trained recruits for the Union army at Springfield. Valued for his previous military experience in the Mexican War and on the West Coast, he accepted the colonelcy of the 21st Illinois Infantry in June 1861, and in August was appointed brigadier-general of volunteers commanding the critical District of Southeast Missouri with headquarters at Cairo, Illinois. Following an unspectacular action against Confederate-held Belmont, Missouri, on November 7, 1861, he gained national attention in the wake of his successful operations against forts Henry and Donelson. His skill as a commander was further confirmed at Shiloh in 1862 and during the Vicksburg Campaign of 1863. His willingness to fight and ability to win impressed Lincoln who ordered him east and appointed him general-in-chief of the Armies of the United States, with the rank of lieutenant-general in the regular army, on March 12, 1864.

A junior engineer officer in the US army before the Civil War, **George G. Meade** was promoted to brigadier-general on August 31, 1861. He was severely wounded during the Seven Days Battles of 1862, but recovered sufficiently to participate at Second Bull Run commanding a brigade of Pennsylvanians in McDowell's III Corps, Army of Virginia. Following the heroic stand his troops made on Henry House Hill to protect the retreating

Lieutenant-General Ulysses S. Grant was fearful that Lee's Army of Northern Virginia might escape south and join forces with Joseph E. Johnston's Army of the Tennessee before he could break through the siege lines at Petersburg. Hence he began his spring offensive against the Confederates in appalling weather on March 27. (Library of Congress LC-DIG-cwpb-06947)

LEFT

Major-General George G. Meade continued to command the Army of the Potomac after Grant became his superior in March 1864. Despite the differences that existed between the two generals, Grant stated in a telegram to Secretary of War Edwin Stanton on May 13, 1864: "Meade has more than met my most sanguine expectations. He and Sherman are the fittest officers for large commands I have come in contact with." (Library of Congress LC-DIG-cwpbh-01199)

RIGHT

In April 1864, Major-General Philip H. Sheridan was appointed to command the Cavalry Corps, Army of the Potomac, and also given responsibility for the Middle Military Division. After destroying much of the Shenandoah Valley and defeating the remnants of Jubal Early's army at Waynesboro on March 2, 1865, he joined Grant south of Petersburg for the final Appomattox Campaign. An independent commander, Sheridan was not under the orders of Meade but subject to Grant alone. (Library of Congress LC-DIG-cwpbh-01009)

Union army, he rose rapidly through the ranks distinguishing himself at South Mountain on September 14, 1862, commanding the 3rd Division, I Corps, Army of the Potomac. Promoted to major-general, he received command of the V Corps, which he led at Chancellorsville during the spring of 1863. He replaced Hooker as commander of the Army of the Potomac on June 28, 1863, and shortly after fought and won a monumental victory at Gettysburg. When Grant was appointed commander of all Union armies in March 1864, Meade felt passed over and offered to resign. However, Grant refused to accept his resignation and established his headquarters with Meade at City Point, Virginia, which caused additional friction between the two generals for the remainder of the war. Meade was incapacitated by a heavy cold throughout most of the Appomattox Campaign.

Nicknamed "Little Phil," **Philip H. Sheridan** held several administrative posts with no mounted experience before being appointed colonel of the 2nd Michigan Cavalry on May 25, 1862. After only eight days he was given command of the 2nd Brigade, Cavalry Division, Army of the Mississippi, being promoted to brigadier-general one month later based on a hard-fought victory at Booneville, Mississippi. He next commanded the 11th Division, Army of the Ohio, and fought well at Perryville, Kentucky, in October 1862. At Stones River, Tennessee, in December 1862 he earned his second star commanding the 3rd Division, Right Wing, XVI Corps, Army of the Cumberland. He then led the 3rd Division, XX Corps at Winchester, Tennessee, and the 2nd Division, IV Corps, at Chickamauga. After earning further distinction during the Chattanooga Campaign, Grant appointed him to command the Cavalry Corps, Army of the Potomac, following which he conducted his Richmond raid between May 9 and 24, which resulted in the defeat and death of Confederate cavalry commander "Jeb" Stuart at Yellow Tavern. From August 1864 through February 1865 he commanded the Army of the Shenandoah, plus the Middle Military Division, during which time he undertook his brilliant Valley Campaign, winning victories at Winchester, Fisher's Hill and Cedar Creek. Following repeated exhortations from Grant to join him outside Petersburg, Sheridan finally moved out of his winter quarters on February 27, 1865, and headed south.

OPPOSING FORCES

CONFEDERATE

By the end of March 1865, the Army of Northern Virginia consisted of about 44,000 infantrymen "present and effective for the field." The cavalry amounted to approximately 5,000 and the artillery 5,000. The Richmond forces under Lieutenant-General Richard S. Ewell numbered 4,000 while what became the Naval Brigade at Drewry's Bluff added a furthur 400 seamen and marines, which brought the total number under Lee's command at the beginning of the Appomattox Campaign to about 58,400. Many of these men were veterans with over three years of battle and campaign experience. About 12 percent were conscripts. Some of the artillery units had spent much of the war performing defensive duty in the trenches around Richmond and Petersburg. The numerical strength of most Confederate units was much reduced by the spring of 1865 with many containing only 200 to 350 men, only a third of which were effective in many cases. For example, on January 30 the 7th Virginia Cavalry contained 346 men on its roll of which only 106 were present for duty.

The main part of Lee's army consisted of I, II and III Corps, under James Longstreet, John B. Gordon and Ambrose P. Hill, respectively; a smaller and newly created IV Corps commanded by Richard H. Anderson (known as Anderson's Corps); and a Cavalry Corps under Fitzhugh Lee. Each of the first three army corps comprised three infantry divisions commanded by a major-general who was supported by a large staff consisting of adjutants, quartermasters, commissaries and surgeons. Anderson's Corps possessed only one division (Johnson's). Each division consisted of four brigades of infantry containing from two to five regiments. Each corps also possessed artillery battalions comprising numerous individual batteries. Fitzhugh Lee's Cavalry Corps also consisted of only three divisions, plus a brigade of horse artillery under Major Preston R. Chew.

Formed in 1862, I Corps was reorganized from the Right Wing of the Army of Northern Virginia and fought in nearly all of the major battles in the Eastern Theater. It returned from hard service in Tennessee to join Lee for the Wilderness Campaign in the spring of 1864 and, following the wounding of Longstreet, had been placed under Richard H. Anderson for much of the early part of the Petersburg Campaign. The smallest in Lee's army, II Corps was formed after Sharpsburg and developed a reputation for hard fighting under its earlier commander Thomas J. "Stonewall" Jackson. It had been led by Jubal Early since May 1864, but he was replaced by John B.

Gordon after Early's humiliating defeat at Waynesboro on March 2, 1865. Formed during the reorganization of Lee's army following the Confederate victory at Chancellorsville, A.P. Hill's III Corps came into being in 1863 and fought under him in many campaigns of the Army of Northern Virginia until he was killed on April 2, 1865. Following this, its troops were merged into I Corps. The IV Corps was organized in late 1864 with Anderson in command following Longstreet's return to I Corps in October of that year. It was combined with the remains of II Corps after defeat at Little Sailor's Creek on April 6, 1865. The Cavalry Corps had been formally established by Major-General J.E.B. Stuart on August 17, 1862. Wade Hampton III took command after Stuart's death at Yellow Tavern on May 11, 1864. Ordered south to assist Johnston in North Carolina at the beginning of April 1865, Hampton was replaced by Fitzhugh Lee.

UNION

By the end of March 1865, the Army of the Potomac consisted of 75,939 men, the Army of the James 27,647, while Sheridan brought two additional cavalry divisions numbering about 9,000, which totaled 112,586. Under the direction of Ulysses S. Grant, the Army of the Potomac, with George G. Meade in tactical command, was composed of the II, V, VI and IX corps. Formed in April 1864 under Major-General Benjamin Butler for the purpose of taking Richmond and Petersburg, the Army of the James was led by Major-General Edward O.C. Ord from December 1864 and consisted of the Defenses of Bermuda Hundred plus XXIV and XXV corps. All of these corps were composed of three infantry divisions plus a brigade of artillery, with the exception of XXV Corps, which had only two infantry divisions.

Commanded by Major-General Andrew A. Humphreys from November 26, 1864, the Army of the Potomac's II Corps was one of the original six provisional army corps established by Lincoln in 1862. Created during the same year, V Corps was led by Major-General Gouverneur K. Warren until his dismissal following a supposed lack of aggressive pursuit of the enemy at Five Forks on April 1, 1865, when he was replaced by Charles Griffin. The VI Corps was under Major-General Horatio G. Wright, having had its commander John Sedgwick killed at Spotsylvania Court House on May 9, 1864. After hard service with Sheridan in the Shenandoah Valley, it returned to the Army of the Potomac in December 1864 and would be assigned a prominent and important part in the final assault on the fortifications of Petersburg in April 1865. Described as "A wandering corps, whose dead lie buried in seven states," IX Corps was originally formed from troops of the Department of the South and from Burnside's Expeditionary Corps for operations in North Carolina. It had served in the Department of the Ohio fighting in Kentucky, Tennessee, and Mississippi before returning east in April 1864 to be placed once more under Burnside. Following that commander's dismissal for the failure of the Petersburg Mine Assault on July 30, 1864, IX Corps served under John G. Parke throughout the Appomattox Campaign.

Created from the X and XVIII corps when the white and black units of the Army of the James were separated on December 3, 1864, the XXIV Corps was initially commanded by Edward O.C. Ord but by January 15 was under the able command of John Gibbon. During the Appomattox Campaign, an Independent Division of troops that had served in the Shenandoah Valley was added to the

Photographed at Appomattox Court House following the Confederate surrender, this group of Union infantrymen is typical of the men that finally defeated the Army of Northern Virginia. Most wear four-button sack coats and narrow-brimmed plug hats. The soldier standing second from left has non-issue dark-colored trousers while the man standing in the back row has the rarely seen heart-shaped badge of XXIV Corps attached to the front of his hat. Their Model 1863 rifle muskets are stacked at their front. (Library of Congress LC-DIG-ppmsca-35159)

1st and 3rd divisions of this corps. Established on the same date, the XXV Corps was composed of African-American units previously belonging to the X and XVIII corps, and was commanded by Major-General Godfrey Weitzel. These were the first Union infantry to occupy Richmond on April 3, 1865.

Originally created under Major-General Robert Patterson in 1861, the second manifestation of the Army of the Shenandoah was organized under Philip H. Sheridan on August 1, 1864; within a three-month period, the army had laid waste to the Shenandoah Valley, which did much to hasten the end of the Civil War. Summoned to join Grant south of the James River, Sheridan's cavalry finally arrived on March 26, 1864, after fighting their way across northern Virginia.

ORDER OF BATTLE

UNION FORCES

ARMY OF THE POTOMAC

Approximately 112,000 men
Commander: Lieutenant-General Ulysses S. Grant, General-in-Chief of the Armies of the United States
Major-General George G.

Meade (tactical command)
Escort
Companies B, F and K, 5th US Cavalry
Headquarters Guard
3rd US Cavalry
Provost Guard (Colonel George N. Macy)
1st Indiana Cavalry (Company K)

1st Massachusetts Cavalry (Companies C and D)
3rd Pennsylvania Cavalry
1st Battalion, 11th US Cavalry
2nd Battalion, 14th US Cavalry
Quartermaster's Guard
Oneida (New York) Cavalry
Engineer Brigade (Brigadier-General Henry W. Benham)

15th New York Engineers (9 companies)
50th New York Engineers
Battalion, US Engineers
Artillery (Brigadier-General Henry J. Hunt, chief of artillery)
Siege train (Colonel Henry L. Abbot)
1st Connecticut Heavy

Artillery

3rd Connecticut Battery

Artillery Reserve (Brigadier-General William Hays)

2nd Maine Battery

3rd Maine Battery

4th Maine Battery

6th Maine Battery

5th Massachusetts Battery

9th Massachusetts Battery

14th Massachusetts Battery

3rd New Jersey Battery

1st New York (Companies C, E, G and L)

12th New York Battery

1st Ohio Battery (Company H)

1st Pennsylvania (Companies B and F)

1st Rhode Island Battery (Company E)

3rd Vermont Battery

5th US (Companies C and I)

II Army Corps (Major-General Andrew A. Humphreys)

1st Division (Brigadier-General Nelson A. Miles)

1st Brigade (Colonel George W. Scott)

26th Michigan

5th New Hampshire (battalion)

2nd New York Heavy Artillery

61st New York

81st Pennsylvania

140th Pennsylvania

2nd Brigade (Colonel Robert Nugent)

28th Massachusetts (5 companies)

63rd New York (6 companies)

69th New York

88th New York (5 companies)

4th New York Heavy Artillery

3rd Brigade (Colonel Henry J. Madill/ Brigadier-General Clinton D. MacDougall)

7th New York

39th New York

52nd New York

111th New York

125th New York

126th New York (battalion)

4th Brigade (Colonel John Ramsey)

64th New York (battalion)

66th New York

53rd Pennsylvania

116th Pennsylvania

145th Pennsylvania

148th Pennsylvania

183rd Pennsylvania

2nd Division (Brigadier-General William Hays, Brigadier-General Francis C. Barlow)

1st Brigade (Colonel William A. Olmsted)

19th Maine

19th Massachusetts

20th Massachusetts

7th Michigan

1st Minnesota (2 companies)

59th New York

152nd New York

184th Pennsylvania

36th Wisconsin

2nd Brigade (Colonel James P. McIvor)

8th New York Heavy Artillery

155th New York

164th New York

170th New York

182nd New York (69th NYNG Artillery)

3rd Brigade (Brigadier-General Thomas A. Smyth, Colonel Daniel Woodall)

14th Connecticut

1st Delaware

12th New Jersey

10th New York (battalion)

108th New York

4th Ohio (4 companies)

69th Pennsylvania

106th Pennsylvania (3 companies)

7th West Virginia (4 companies)

Unattached: 2nd Company Minnesota Sharpshooters

3rd Division (Brigadier-General Gershom Mott, Brigadier-General P. Régis de Trobriand)

1st Brigade (Brigadier-General P. Regis de Trobriand, Colonel Russell B.

Shepherd)

20th Indiana

1st Maine Heavy Artillery

40th New York

73rd New York

86th New York

124th New York

99th Pennsylvania

110th Pennsylvania

2nd Brigade (Brigadier-General Byron R. Pierce)

17th Maine

1st Massachusetts Heavy Artillery

5th Michigan

93rd New York

57th Pennsylvania

105th Pennsylvania

141st Pennsylvania

3rd Brigade (Colonel Robert McAllister)

11th Massachusetts

7th New Jersey

8th New Jersey

11th New Jersey

120th New York

Artillery Brigade (Major John G. Hazard)

10th Massachusetts

1st New Hampshire (Battery M)

2nd New Jersey Battery

11th New York Battery

4th New York Heavy Artillery (Battery C)

4th New York Heavy Artillery (Battery L)

1st Rhode Island (Battery B)

4th US (Company K)

V Army Corps (Major-General Gouverneur K. Warren, Brigadier-General Charles Griffin)

Escort

4th Pennsylvania Cavalry (Company C)

Provost Guard

104th New York Infantry

1st Division (Brigadier-General Charles Griffin, Brigadier-General Joseph J. Bartlett)

1st Brigade (Brigadier-General Joshua L. Chamberlain)

185th New York

198th Pennsylvania

2nd Brigade (Colonel Edgar M. Gregory)

187th New York

188th New York

189th New York

3rd Brigade (Brigadier-General Joseph J. Bartlett)

1st Maine Sharpshooters

20th Maine

32nd Massachusetts

1st Michigan

16th Michigan

83rd Pennsylvania

91st Pennsylvania

118th Pennsylvania

155th Pennsylvania

2nd Division (Brigadier-General Romeyn B. Ayres)

1st Brigade (Colonel Frederick Winthrop)

5th New York (Veteran)

15th New York Heavy Artillery

140th New York

146th New York

2nd Brigade (Colonel David L. Stanton)

1st Maryland

4th Maryland

7th Maryland

8th Maryland

3rd Brigade (Colonel James Gwyn)

3rd Delaware

4th Delaware

8th Delaware (3 companies)

157th Pennsylvania (4 companies)

190th Pennsylvania

191st Pennsylvania

210th Pennsylvania

3rd Division (Brigadier-General Samuel W. Crawford)

1st Brigade (Colonel John A. Kellogg)

91st New York

6th Wisconsin

7th Wisconsin

2nd Brigade (Brigadier-General Henry Baxter)

16th Maine

39th Massachusetts

97th New York

11th Pennsylvania

107th Pennsylvania

3rd Brigade (Colonel Richard
Coulter)
94th New York
95th New York
147th New York
56th Pennsylvania
88th Pennsylvania
121st Pennsylvania
142nd Pennsylvania
Unattached: 1st Battalion New
York Sharpshooters
Artillery Brigade (Colonel
Charles S. Wainwright)
1st New York (Batteries B,
D and H)
15th New York Heavy
Artillery (Battery M)
4th US (Battery B)
5th US (Batteries D and G)

**VI Army Corps (Major-
General Horatio G. Wright)**
Escort
21st Pennsylvania Cavalry
(Company E)
**1st Division (Brigadier-
General Frank Wheaton)**
1st Brigade (Colonel William
H. Penrose)
1st and 4th New Jersey
(battalion)
2nd New Jersey
(2 companies)
3rd New Jersey
(1 company)
10th New Jersey
15th New Jersey
40th New Jersey
2nd Brigade (Colonel Joseph
E. Hamblin)
2nd Connecticut Heavy
Artillery
65th New York
121st New York
95th Pennsylvania
3rd Brigade (Colonel Oliver
Edwards)
37th Massachusetts
49th Pennsylvania
82nd Pennsylvania
119th Pennsylvania
2nd Rhode Island
5th Wisconsin
**2nd Division (Brigadier-
General George W. Getty)**
1st Brigade (Colonel James
M. Warner)
62nd New York

93rd Pennsylvania
98th Pennsylvania
102nd Pennsylvania
139th Pennsylvania
2nd Brigade (Brigadier-General
Lewis A. Grant)
2nd Vermont
3rd and 4th Vermont
5th Vermont
6th Vermont
1st Vermont Heavy
Artillery
3rd Brigade (Colonel Thomas
W. Hyde)
1st Maine
43rd New York
(5 companies)
49th New York
(5 companies)
77th New York
(5 companies)
122nd New York

**3rd Division (Brigadier-
General Truman
Seymour)**
1st Brigade (Colonel William
S. Truex)
14th New Jersey
106th New York
151st New York
(5 companies)
87th Pennsylvania
10th Vermont
2nd Brigade (Colonel J. Warren
Keifer)
6th Maryland
9th New York Heavy
Artillery
110th Ohio
122nd Ohio
126th Ohio
67th Pennsylvania
138th Pennsylvania
Artillery Brigade (Captain
Andrew Cowan)
1st New Jersey (Battery A)
1st New York
3rd New York (Battery L)
9th New York Heavy
Artillery
1st Rhode Island
(Battery G)
1st Rhode Island
(Battery H)
5th US (Battery E)
1st Vermont Heavy
Artillery (Battery D)

**IX Army Corps (Major-
General John G. Parke)**
Provost Guard
79th New York
**1st Division (Brigadier-General
Orlando B. Wilcox)**
1st Brigade (Colonel Samuel
Harriman)
8th Michigan
27th Michigan
109th New York
51st Pennsylvania
37th Wisconsin
38th Wisconsin
2nd Brigade (Lieutenant-
Colonel Ralph Ely)
1st Michigan
Sharpshooters
2nd Michigan
20th Michigan
46th New York
60th Ohio
50th Pennsylvania
3rd Brigade (Lieutenant-
Colonel Gilbert P.
Robinson)
3rd Maryland Battalion
29th Massachusetts
57th Massachusetts
59th Massachusetts
18th New Hampshire
14th New York Heavy
Artillery
100th Pennsylvania
Acting Engineers:
17th Michigan
**2nd Division (Brigadier-
General Robert B. Potter,
Brigadier-General Simon
G. Griffin)**
1st Brigade (Colonel John
I. Curtin)
35th Massachusetts
36th Massachusetts
58th Massachusetts
39th New Jersey
51st New York
45th Pennsylvania
48th Pennsylvania
7th Rhode Island
2nd Brigade (Brigadier-General
Simon G. Griffin)
31st Maine
2nd Maryland
56th Massachusetts
6th New Hampshire
9th New Hampshire

11th New Hampshire
179th New York
186th New York
17th Vermont
**3rd Division (Brigadier-
General John F.
Hartranft)**
1st Brigade (Lieutenant-Colonel
W. H. McCall)
200th Pennsylvania
208th Pennsylvania
209th Pennsylvania
2nd Brigade (Colonel Joseph
A. Mathews)
205th Pennsylvania
207th Pennsylvania
211th Pennsylvania
Artillery Brigade (Colonel John
C. Tidball)
7th Maine
11th Massachusetts
19th New York
27th New York
34th New York
Cavalry
2nd Pennsylvania
Independent Brigade (Colonel
Charles H.T. Collis)
1st Massachusetts Cavalry
61st Massachusetts
80th New York
(20th Militia)
68th Pennsylvania
114th Pennsylvania

**Cavalry (Major-General
Philip H. Sheridan)
Army of the Shenandoah
(Brigadier-General Wesley
Merritt)**
**1st Division (Brigadier-
General Thomas C. Devin)**
1st Brigade (Colonel Peter
Stagg)
1st Michigan
5th Michigan
6th Michigan
7th Michigan
2nd Brigade (Colonel Charles
L. Fitzhugh)
6th New York
9th New York
19th New York (1st New
York Dragoons)
17th Pennsylvania
20th Pennsylvania
3rd (Reserve) Brigade
(Brigadier-General Alfred

Gibbs)
2nd Massachusetts
6th Pennsylvania
(6 companies)
1st US
5th US
6th US
Artillery
4th US (Batteries C and E)

3rd Division (Brigadier-General George A. Custer)
1st Brigade (Colonel Alexander C. M. Pennington)
1st Connecticut
3rd New Jersey
2nd New York
2nd Ohio
2nd Brigade (Colonel William Wells)
8th New York
15th New York
1st Vermont
3rd Brigade (Colonel Henry Capehart)
1st New York
1st West Virginia
2nd West Virginia
3rd West Virginia

2nd Division, Army of the Potomac (Major-General George Crook)
1st Brigade (Brigadier-General Henry E. Davies)
1st New Jersey
10th New York
24th New York
1st Pennsylvania (5 companies)
2nd US Artillery (Battery A)
2nd Brigade (Colonel J. Irvin Gregg)
4th Pennsylvania
8th Pennsylvania
16th Pennsylvania
21st Pennsylvania
1st US Artillery (Batteries H and I)
3rd Brigade (Colonel Charles H. Smith)
1st Maine
2nd New York Mounted Rifles
6th Ohio
13th Ohio

ARMY OF THE JAMES (MAJOR-GENERAL EDWARD O.C. ORD)
Headquarters Guard
3rd Pennsylvania Artillery (Batteries D and I)
Engineers
1st New York
Pontoniers
3rd Massachusetts Artillery (Battery I)
Unattached Cavalry
4th Massachusetts (Companies I, L and M)
5th Massachusetts (colored)
7th New York (1st Mounted Rifles)
Defenses of Bermuda Hundred (Major-General George L. Hartsuff)
Infantry Division (Brigadier-General Edward Ferrero)
1st Brigade (Brevet Brigadier-General Gilbert H. McKibbin)
41st New York
103rd New York
2nd Pennsylvania Heavy Artillery
104th Pennsylvania
2nd Brigade (Colonel George C. Kibbe)
6th New York Heavy Artillery
10th New York Heavy Artillery
33rd New York
Artillery
13th New York Heavy Artillery (Batteries A and H)
7th New York
3rd Pennsylvania Heavy Artillery (Batteries E and M)
Separate Brigade (Brigadier-General Joseph B. Carr)
Fort Pocahontas (Lieutenant-Colonel Ashbel W. Angel)
38th New Jersey (4 companies)
20th New York Cavalry (Company D)
16th New York Heavy Artillery (Batteries E and I)
184th New York
Harrison's Landing (Colonel Wardwell G. Robinson)
184th New York
1st US Colored Cavalry

(Company I)
Fort Powhatan (Colonel William J. Sewell)
38th New Jersey (6 companies)
20th New York Cavalry (Company F)
Detachment 3rd Pennsylvania Heavy Artillery
1st US Colored Cavalry (Company E)
XXIV Army Corps (Major-General John Gibbon)
Headquarters Guard
4th Massachusetts Cavalry (Companies F and K)
1st Division (Brigadier-General Robert S. Foster)
1st Brigade (Colonel Thomas O. Osborn)
39th Illinois
62nd Ohio
67th Ohio
85th Pennsylvania (Company G)
199th Pennsylvania
3rd Brigade (Colonel George B. Dandy)
10th Connecticut
11th Maine
24th Massachusetts
100th New York
206th Pennsylvania
4th Brigade (Colonel Harrison S. Fairchild)
8th Maine
89th New York
148th New York
158th New York
55th Pennsylvania
3rd Division (Brigadier-General Charles Devens, Jr)
1st Brigade (Colonel Edward H. Ripley)
11th Connecticut
13th New Hampshire
81st New York
98th New York
139th New York
19th Wisconsin
2nd Brigade (Colonel Michael T. Donohoe)
8th Connecticut
5th Maryland
10th New Hampshire
12th New Hampshire

96th New York
118th New York
9th Vermont
3rd Brigade (Colonel Samuel H. Roberts)
21st Connecticut
40th Massachusetts
2nd New Hampshire
58th Pennsylvania
188th Pennsylvania
Independent Division (Brigadier-General John W. Turner)
1st Brigade (Lieutenant-Colonel Andrew Potter)
34th Massachusetts
116th Ohio
123rd Ohio
2nd Brigade (Colonel William B. Curtis)
23rd Illinois
54th Pennsylvania
12th West Virginia
3rd Brigade (Colonel Thomas M. Harris)
10th West Virginia
11th West Virginia
15th West Virginia
Artillery (Major Charles C. Abell)
3rd New York (Batteries E, H, K and M)
17th New York
1st Pennsylvania (Battery A)
1st Rhode Island (Battery F)
1st US (Battery B)
4th US (Battery L)
5th US (Batteries A and F)
XXV Army Corps (Major-General Godfrey Weitzel)
Provost Guard
4th Massachusetts Cavalry (Companies E and H)
1st Division (Colored Troops) (Brigadier-General August V. Kautz)
1st Brigade (Colonel Alonzo G. Draper)
22nd US
36th US
38th US
118th US
2nd Brigade (Brigadier-General Edward A. Wild)
29th Connecticut
9th US
115th US

117th US

3rd Brigade (Brigadier-General
   Henry G. Thomas)

19th US

23rd US

43rd US

114th US

Attached Brigade (Colonel
   Charles S. Russell)

10th US

28th US

Cavalry

2nd US Colored

**2nd Division (Brigadier-
General William Birney)**

1st Brigade (Colonel James
   Shaw, Jr)

7th US

109th US

116th US

2nd Brigade (Colonel Ulysses
   Doubleday)

8th US

41st US

45th US

127th US

3rd Brigade (Colonel William
   W. Woodward)

29th US

31st US

**Artillery Brigade (Captain
Loomis L. Langdon)**

1st Connecticut

4th New Jersey

5th New Jersey

1st Pennsylvania
   (Battery E)

3rd Rhode Island
   (Battery C)

1st US (Batteries D and M)

4th US (Battery D)

**Cavalry Division (Brigadier-
General Ranald S.
Mackenzie)**

1st Brigade (Colonel Robert
   M. West)

20th New York (Battery G)

5th Pennsylvania

2nd Brigade (Colonel Samuel
   P. Spear)

1st District of Columbia
   (battalion)

1st Maryland

11th Pennsylvania

Artillery

4th Wisconsin

CONFEDERATE FORCES

ARMY OF NORTHERN VIRGINIA

Approximately 58,400 men
General Robert E. Lee, General-
   in-Chief of Confederate
   forces

Provost Guard

1st Virginia Battalion and
   44th Virginia Battalion
   (Company B)

Escort

39th Virginia Battalion

**Engineer Troops (Colonel T.
M. R. Talcott)**

1st Regiment

2nd Regiment

**I Army Corps (Lieutenant-
General James Longstreet)**

**Pickett's Division (Major-
General George E. Pickett)**

Steuart's Brigade (Brigadier-
   General George H. Steuart)

9th Virginia

14th Virginia

38th Virginia

53rd Virginia

57th Virginia

Corse's Brigade (Brigadier-
   General Montgomery D.
   Corse)

15th Virginia

17th Virginia

29th Virginia

30th Virginia

32nd Virginia

Hunton's Brigade (Brigadier-
   General Eppa Hunton)

8th Virginia

18th Virginia

19th Virginia

28th Virginia

56th Virginia

Terry's Brigade (Brigadier-
   General William R. Terry)

1st Virginia

3rd Virginia

7th Virginia

11th Virginia

4th Virginia

**Field's Division (Major-
General Charles W. Field)**

Perry's (late Law's) Brigade

(Brigadier-General William
   F. Perry)

4th Alabama

15th Alabama

44th Alabama

47th Alabama

48th Alabama

Anderson's Brigade (Brigadier-
   General George T.
   Anderson)

7th Georgia

8th Georgia

9th Georgia

11th Georgia

59th Georgia

Benning's Brigade (Brigadier-
   General Henry L. Benning)

2nd Georgia

15th Georgia

17th Georgia

20th Georgia

Gregg's Brigade (Colonel R. M.
   Powell)

3rd Arkansas

1st Texas

4th Texas

5th Texas

Bratton's Brigade (Brigadier-
   General John Bratton)

1st South Carolina

5th South Carolina

6th South Carolina

2nd South Carolina Rifles

Palmetto (South Carolina)
   Sharpshooters

**Kershaw's Division (Major-
General Joseph B.
Kershaw)**

Du Bose's Brigade (Brigadier-
   General Dudley
   M. Du Bose)

16th Georgia

18th Georgia

24th Georgia

3rd Georgia Battalion
   Sharpshooters

Cobb's Georgia Legion

Phillips's Georgia Legion

Humphreys's Brigade (Colonel
   W.H. Fitzgerald)

13th Mississippi

17th Mississippi

18th Mississippi

21st Mississippi

Simms's Brigade (Brigadier-
   General James P. Simms)

10th Georgia

50th Georgia

51st Georgia

53rd Georgia

**Artillery (Brigadier-General
E.P. Alexander)**

Haskell's Battalion (Major John
   C. Haskell)

Flanner's North Carolina
   Battery

Ramsey's North Carolina
   Battery

Garden's South Carolina
   Battery

Lamkin's Virginia Battery

Huger's Battalion (Major Tyler
   C. Jordan)

Moody's Louisiana Battery

Ficking's South Carolina
   Battery

Parker's Virginia Battery

Smith's Virginia Battery

Taylor's Virginia Battery

Woolfolk Virginia Battery

**II Army Corps (Lieutenant-
General John B. Gordon)**

**Grimes's (late Rodes')
Division (Major-General
Bryan Grimes)**

Battle's Brigade (Colonel Edwin
   L. Hobson)

3rd Alabama

5th Alabama

6th Alabama

12th Alabama

61st Alabama

Grimes's Brigade (Colonel D.G.
   Cowand)

32nd North Carolina

43rd North Carolina

45th North Carolina

53rd North Carolina

2nd North Carolina
   Battalion

Cox's Brigade (Brigadier-
   General William R. Cox)

1st North Carolina

2nd North Carolina

3rd North Carolina

4th North Carolina

14th North Carolina

30th North Carolina

Cook's Brigade (Colonel Edwin
   A. Nash)

4th Georgia

12th Georgia

21st Georgia
44th Georgia
Patterson's Georgia Battery
Archer's Battalion (Lieutenant-
Colonel F.H. Archer)
3rd Battalion Virginia
Reserves
44th Battalion Virginia
Reserves

Early's Division (Brigadier-General James A. Walker)
Johnston's Brigade (Colonel
John W. Lea)
5th North Carolina
12th North Carolina
20th North Carolina
23rd North Carolina
1st North Carolina
Battalion
Lewis's Brigade (Brigadier-
General William Lewis/
Captain John Beard)
6th North Carolina
21st North Carolina
54th North Carolina
57th North Carolina
Walker's (late Pegram's) Brigade
(Major Henry Kyd
Douglas)
13th Virginia
31st Virginia
49th Virginia
52nd Virginia
58th Virginia

Gordon's Division (Brigadier-General Clement A. Evans)
Evans's Brigade (Colonel J.H.
Lowe)
13th Georgia
26th Georgia
31st Georgia
38th Georgia
60th and 61st Georgia
9th Georgia Battalion
Artillery
12th Georgia Battalion
Artillery
18th Georgia Battalion
Artillery
Terry's Brigade (Brigadier-
General William R. Terry/
Colonel Joseph Mayo)
2nd Virginia
4th Virginia
5th Virginia

10th Virginia
21st Virginia
23rd Virginia
25th Virginia
27th Virginia
33rd Virginia
37th Virginia
42nd Virginia
44th Virginia
48th Virginia
York's Brigade (Colonel Eugene
Waggaman)
1st Louisiana
2nd Louisiana
5th Louisiana
6th Louisiana
7th Louisiana
8th Louisiana
9th Louisiana
10th Louisiana
14th Louisiana

Artillery (Brigadier-General Armistead L. Long)
Braxton's Battalion (Lieutenant-
Colonel Carter M. Braxton)
Carpenter's Virginia Battery
Cooper's Virginia Battery
Hardwicke's Virginia
Battery
Cutshaw's Battalion (Captain
C.W. Fry)
Reese's Alabama Battery
Carter's Virginia Battery
Montgomery's Virginia
Battery
Fry's Virginia Battery
Garber's Virginia Battery
Jones's Virginia Battery
Hardaway's Battalion
(Lieutenant-Colonel Robert
A. Hardaway)
Dance's Virginia Battery
Graham's Virginia Battery
Griffin's Virginia Battery
Smith's Virginia Battery
Johnson's Battalion
(Lieutenant-Colonel
Marmaduke Johnson)
Clutter's Virginia Battery
Pollock's Virginia Battery
Lightfoot's Battalion
Caroline Artillery
Nelson Artillery
Surry Artillery
Stark's Battalion (Lieutenant-
Colonel Alexander W. Stark)

Green's Louisiana Battery
French's Virginia Battery
Armistead's Virginia Battery

III Army Corps (Lieutenant-General Ambrose P. Hill)
Heth's Division (Major-General Henry Heth)
Davis's Brigade (Brigadier-
General Joseph R. Davis)
1st Confederate Battalion
2nd Mississippi
11th Mississippi
26th Mississippi
42nd Mississippi
Cooke's Brigade (Brigadier-
General John R. Cooke)
15th North Carolina
27th North Carolina
46th North Carolina
48th North Carolina
55th North Carolina
MacRae's Brigade (Brigadier-
General William MacRae)
11th North Carolina
26th North Carolina
44th North Carolina
47th North Carolina
52nd North Carolina
McComb's Brigade (Brigadier-
General William McComb)
2nd Maryland Battalion
1st Tennessee (Provisional
Army)
7th Tennessee
14th Tennessee
17th and 23rd Tennessee
25th and 44th Tennessee
63rd Tennessee

Wilcox's Division (Major-General Cadmus M. Wilcox)
Thomas's Brigade (Brigadier-
General Edward L. Thomas)
14th Georgia
35th Georgia
45th Georgia
49th Georgia
Lane's Brigade (Brigadier-
General James H. Lane)
18th North Carolina
28th North Carolina
33rd North Carolina
37th North Carolina
McGowan's Brigade (Brigadier-
General Samuel McGowan)
1st South Carolina

(Provisional Army)
12th South Carolina
13th South Carolina
14th South Carolina
Orr's South Carolina Rifles
Scales's Brigade (Colonel
Joseph H. Hyman)
13th North Carolina
16th North Carolina
22nd North Carolina
34th North Carolina
38th North Carolina

Mahone's Division (Major-General William Mahone)
Forney's Brigade (Brigadier-
General William H. Forney)
8th Alabama
9th Alabama
10th Alabama
11th Alabama
13th Alabama
14th Alabama
Weisiger's Brigade (Brigadier-
General David A. Weisiger)
6th Virginia
12th Virginia
16th Virginia
41st Virginia
61st Virginia
Harris's Brigade (Brigadier-
General N.H. Harris)
12th Mississippi
16th Mississippi
19th Mississippi
48th Mississippi
Sorrel's Brigade (Colonel
George E. Tayloe)
3rd Georgia
22nd Georgia
48th Georgia
64th Georgia
2nd Georgia Battalion
10th Georgia Battalion
Finegan's Brigade (Colonel
David Lang)
2nd Florida
5th Florida
8th Florida
9th Florida
10th Florida
11th Florida

Artillery (Brigadier-General R.L. Walker)
McIntosh's Battalion
Hurt's Alabama Battery
Owens's Louisiana Battery

Chew's Maryland Battery

Chamberlayne's Virginia Battery

Price's Virginia Battery

Donald's Virginia Battery

Poague's Battalion (Lieutenant-Colonel William T. Poague)

Richard's Mississippi Battery

Williams's North Carolina Battery

Johnston's Virginia Battery

Utterback's Virginia Battery

Perrick's Virginia Battery

13th Virginia Battalion

Otey Battery

Ringgold Battery

Richardson's Battalion (Lieutenant-Colonel Charles Richardson)

Landry's Louisiana Battery

Moore's Virginia Battery

Grandy's Virginia Battery

Pegram's Battalion (Colonel William J. Pegram)

Gregg's South Carolina Battery

Cayce's Virginia Battery

Ellett's Virginia Battery

Brander's Virginia Battery

Anderson's Corps (IV Corps) (Lieutenant-General Richard H. Anderson)

Johnson's Division (Major-General Bushrod R. Johnson)

Wise's Brigade (Brigadier-General Henry A. Wise)

26th Virginia

34th Virginia

46th Virginia

59th Virginia

Wallace's Brigade (Brigadier-General W.H. Wallace)

17th South Carolina

18th South Carolina

22nd South Carolina

23rd South Carolina

26th South Carolina

Holcombe South Carolina Legion

Moody's Brigade (Brigadier-General Young M. Moody)

41st Alabama

43rd Alabama

59th Alabama

60th Alabama

23rd Alabama Battalion

Ransom's Brigade (Brigadier-General Matthew W. Ransom)

24th North Carolina

25th North Carolina

35th North Carolina

49th North Carolina

56th North Carolina

Artillery (Colonel H. P. Jones)

Blount's Battalion

Slaten's Georgia Battery

Cumming's North Carolina Battery

Miller's Virginia Battery

Young's Virginia Battery

Coit's Battalion

Bradford's Mississippi Battery

Pegram's Virginia Battery

Wright's Virginia Battery

Stribling's Battalion

Dickerson's Virginia Battery

Marshall's Virginia Battery

Macon's Virginia Battery

Sullivan's Virginia Battery

Smith's Battalion (Captain William F. Dement)

1st Maryland Battery

Johnston's Virginia Battery

Neblett's Virginia Battery

Drewry's Virginia Battery

Kevill's Virginia Battery

Cavalry Corps (Major-General Wade Hampton, Major-General Fitzhugh Lee)

Lee's Division (Brigadier-General Thomas T. Munford)

Munford's Brigade

1st Virginia

2nd Virginia

3rd Virginia

4th Virginia

Payne's Brigade (Brigadier-General William H. Payne)

5th Virginia

6th Virginia

8th Virginia

36th Virginia Battalion

Gary's Brigade (Brigadier-General Martin W. Gary)

7th Georgia

7th South Carolina

Hampton's Legion Mounted Infantry

24th Virginia

W.H.F. Lee's Division (Major-General Willam Henry Fitzhugh "Rooney" Lee)

Barringer's Brigade (Brigadier-General Rufus Barringer)

1st North Carolina

2nd North Carolina

3rd North Carolina

5th North Carolina

Beale's Brigade (Captain S.H. Burt)

9th Virginia

10th Virginia

13th Virginia

14th Virginia

Roberts's Brigade (Brigadier-General William P. Roberts)

4th North Carolina

16th North Carolina Battalion

Rosser's Division (Major-General Thomas L. Rosser)

Dearing's Brigade (Brigadier-General James Dearing)

7th Virginia

11th Virginia

12th Virginia

35th Virginia Battalion

McCausland's Brigade (Brigadier-General John McCausland)

16th Virginia

17th Virginia

21st Virginia

22nd Virginia

Artillery (Lieutenant-Colonel R.B. Chew)

Chew's Battalion

Graham's Virginia Battery

McGregor's Virginia Battery

Breathed's Battalion (Major James Breathed)

P.P. Johnston's Virginia Battery

Shoemaker's Virginia Battery

Thomson's Virginia Battery

Department of Richmond (Lieutenant-General Richard S. Ewell / Lieutenant-Colonel Thomas J. Spencer)

G.W.C. Lee's Division (Major-General G.W. Custis Lee)

Barton's Brigade (Brigadier-General Seth M. Barton)

22nd Virginia Battalion

25th Virginia Battalion

40th Virginia

47th and 50th Virginia

Moore's Brigade (Brigadier-General Patrick T. Moore)

3rd Local Defense Troops

1st Virginia Reserves

2nd Virginia Reserves

1st Virginia Battalion Reserves

2nd Virginia Battalion Reserves

Artillery Brigade (Colonel Stapleton Crutchfield)

10th Virginia Battalion Heavy Artillery

18th Virginia Battalion Heavy Artillery

20th Virginia Battalion Heavy Artillery

Chaffin's Bluff Garrison (Major Robert Stiles)

18th Georgia Battalion

Drewry's Bluff (artillery acting as infantry) (Major F.W. Smith)

Young's Howitzers

Johnston's Heavy Artillery

Lunenburg Heavy Artillery

Pamunkey Heavy Artillery

Southside Heavy Artillery

Chaffin's Bluff (Lieutenant Colonel J.M. Maury)

Naval Brigade (Commodore John R. Tucker)

Marines (Captain John D. Simms)

Department of North Carolina and Southern Virginia

First Military District (Brigadier-General Henry A. Wise)

Petersburg (Major W.H. Ker)

3rd Battalion Virginia Reserves

44th Virginia Battalion

Hood's Battalion Operatives

Second Class Militia

Independent Signal Corps

OPPOSING PLANS

Following the meeting at City Point, Grant determined to begin his spring offensive during the night of March 27, 1865, when Foster's and Turner's divisions of Gibbon's XXIV Corps, Birney's division of the XXV Corps, and one small division of cavalry under Brigadier-General Ranald S. Mackenzie, Ord's Army of the James, would leave the siege lines around Richmond, cross the James River and march towards Petersburg. The remainder of the Army of the James, under the direction of Major-General Godfrey Weitzel, would continue to hold the lines southeast of Richmond. In the Petersburg lines the IX Corps under Major-General John G. Parke would hold the siege lines east and south of Petersburg, while Major-General Horatio G. Wright's VI Corps maintained its position to the southwest of the city.

Once these troops had arrived south of Petersburg, Major-General Alexander A. Humphreys's II Corps, together with Major-General Gouverneur K. Warren's V Corps, would extend the Union lines southeast of Petersburg towards Dinwiddie Court House on the Boydton Plank Road. As Humphreys's corps moved left, Ord's infantry were to replace Humphreys's men in the trenches. From the Boydton Plank Road, Humphreys and Warren would push back the extreme right wing of the Confederate defenses towards the Southside Railroad. Accompanying the infantry, Sheridan's cavalry would then destroy the Southside and Richmond & Danville railroads, thereby cutting off the last two Confederate rail lifelines and forcing the Confederates to either capitulate or retreat.

In order for this plan to succeed, Ord's troops had to depart the Richmond lines and march nearly 40 miles (65km) along the periphery of the Petersburg lines without being detected by the Confederates. If this relocation of Union troops was discovered by Lee, he might order Longstreet's corps south from the Richmond area to reinforce the Confederate right flank at Petersburg, thus countering any forthcoming Union attack.

With the realization that Grant could envelope his lines to the west of Petersburg, Lee decided as early as February 21, 1865 to prepare for the evacuation of his troops from the trenches around that city and Richmond, and to concentrate them at or near Burkeville Junction where the Richmond & Danville and Southside railroads connected. This, he advised Secretary of War John C. Breckinridge, would retain communication with the north and south of the Confederacy as long as practicable. He also suggested that Lynchburg might be the most advantageous place to deposit stores from Richmond. This, he concluded, was "a most difficult point at this time to decide, and the place may have to be changed by circumstances."

Meanwhile, in an attempt to force Grant to abandon his movement on the Confederate right flank, Lee permitted his II Corps commander, Major-General John B. Gordon, to take the offensive on March 25, 1865 and attack the Federal lines east of Petersburg in the vicinity of Fort Stedman. If this plan worked, Grant might possibly be forced to shorten or abandon his lines west of the city, which would enable Lee to shorten his lines in that area also, and send a portion of his troops south to assist Johnston in North Carolina. Unfortunately, after initial success Gordon's attack was repulsed by a powerful Union counterattack with the loss of about 4,000 irreplaceable Confederate infantry, consisting of 600 killed, 2,400 wounded, and 1,000 missing or captured. The last major offensive action of the Army of Northern Virginia, the Battle of Fort Stedman was a disaster for Lee. He had weakened his defenses and a Union breakthrough was now only a matter of time.

THE CAMPAIGN

THE FALL OF PETERSBURG AND RICHMOND, MARCH 29–APRIL 3

The Petersburg area was lashed with heavy rains during the last few days of March 1865. As a result, the creeks were swollen beyond their banks and roads were reduced to a quagmire. In his report on the campaign, Major-General Gouverneur K. Warren stated: "The country in which we were to operate was of the forest kind common to Virginia, being well watered by swampy streams. The surface is level and the soil clayey or sandy, and, where these mix together, like quicksand. The soil, after the frosts of winter first leave it, is very light and soft, and hoofs and wheels find but little support." Such conditions slowed the progress of infantry and cavalry, and limited the type and amount of artillery that could be used.

Despite the appalling conditions, Ord's Army of the James completed their march from the Richmond area to relieve II Corps in the trenches southwest of Petersburg without detection. In his report of the operation, Major-General John Gibbon stated simply: "The troops marched all night and all the next day, getting into camp near Fort Siebert [about 3 miles, or 5km, from the Petersburg frontline trenches] about sundown on the 28th, performing one of the most remarkable marches on record, with very few stragglers." The intelligence failure that led to his not detecting in a timely manner the movement of Ord's troops may be considered one of the more serious errors of Robert E. Lee's military career.

Spearheading Grant's offensive towards Dinwiddie Court House was Warren's V Corps. The first objective of the infantry was the Boydton Plank Road, while Sheridan was to raid the Southside and Richmond & Danville railroads via Dinwiddie Court House. The advance of V Corps and Sheridan's cavalry began at precisely 3 a.m. on March 29, 1865, while II Corps did not move until 6 a.m., having been relieved by Gibbon's XXIV Corps. Crossing Hatcher's Run via the Old Stage Road, V Corps reached the intersection of the Vaughan and Quaker roads. About noon it was ordered to move north up the Quaker Road to Gravelly Run. The cavalry pushed farther west towards Dinwiddie Court House despite the atrocious road conditions, from which point they headed north in the direction of the Southside Railroad. According to Captain Frederick C. Newhall, 6th Pennsylvania Cavalry, who served as a staff officer with Sheridan, they had "labored on hopefully, every man for himself and his horse." Due to the state of the roads, they did not reach the Court House until about 5 p.m. following which Sheridan posted pickets along the three main approach roads to guard against enemy patrols.

The II Corps crossed Hatcher's Run via the Vaughan Road and by evening had halted and thrown up breastworks with its right wing near Dabney's Mill and left near the Gravelly Meeting-House on the Quaker Road. In taking this position and making contact with elements of V Corps, Humphreys's troops encountered little opposition, meeting only a small force in rifle-pits, which was quickly driven out. However, Warren's V Corps was delayed by having to build two temporary wooden bridges over Gravelly Run in place of the destroyed one. At the head of its column, 1st Division (V Corps) was attacked about 3.20 p.m. near the Lewis house by elements of Bushrod Johnson's Division (IV Corps). Although he encountered fierce opposition, Chamberlain was reinforced and by about 5 p.m. had driven the Confederates back to the Boydton Plank Road. Just before dusk, Lieutenant-General Richard Anderson ordered Johnson to fall back to the breastworks along the White

Accompanied by his staff, divisional and brigade commanders, Sheridan questions an African-American at Dinwiddie Court House on March 29, 1865. Earlier that day, his cavalry had seized that place as part of the flanking movement designed to force Lee's army out of its entrenchments around Petersburg. (*Personal Memoirs of P.H. Sheridan*)

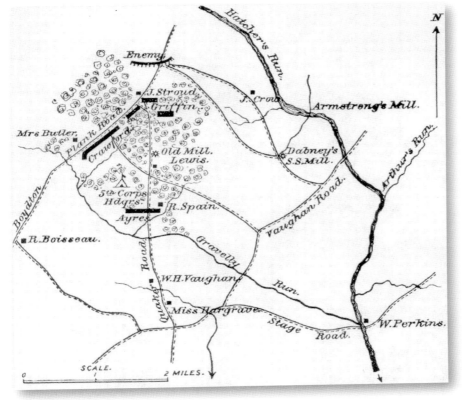

This map from the *Official Records* shows the area over which the Union II and V Corps advanced on March 29, and the final position of the three divisions of V Corps after it had seized the Boydton Plank Road by dusk that day. The capture of that road would serve as the springboard to advance on the White Oak Road, Five Forks, and the Southside Railroad during the next few days. (Author's collection)

Oak Road. As a result, V Corps secured the Boydton Plank Road and had a springboard from which to seize the White Oak Road and Five Forks.

That evening it began to rain again. Staff officer Captain Newhall recalled that it was first "a Scotch mist, then unsteady showers, and then a pour, as if the equinox, hurrying through the elements, had kicked over the water-buckets." Undeterred by the foul weather, Grant became even more determined to press home his planned attack, still driven by the fear that Lee might evacuate his lines and escape south. Thus, he sent a dispatch to Sheridan countermanding his orders to raid the Southside and Richmond & Danville railroads and directing him instead to seize Five Forks and turn the Confederate right flank. Warren and Humphreys were directed to act in support.

On the other side of the siege lines, Lee sent an urgent telegram to the Confederate Secretary of War: "The enemy crossed Hatcher's Run this morning at Monk's Neck Bridge with a large force of cavalry, infantry, & artillery, and tonight his left extended to Dinwiddie Court House." He next ordered the division of Major-General George E. Pickett (I Corps) across the Appomattox River and southwest of Petersburg via the Southside Railroad to Sutherland's Station. Deducing that the Federals would probably move via Dinwiddie Court House to Five Forks in order to flank his army, Lee extended his defenses a further 4 miles (6km) west. Disembarking from the cars and slogging through drenching rain, Pickett's infantry was in hastily prepared breastworks and rifle-pits along the White Oak Road on the extreme right of the Confederate line by daybreak on March 30. Lee also ordered McGowan's South Carolina brigade (Wilcox's Division, III Corps) to move west from the trenches in Hill's sector to man the line at Burgess Mill on Hatcher's Run. Lacking replacement troops, the brigades of Lane (Wilcox's Division) and McComb (Heth's Division) on either side of the gap created by McGowan were stretched even more thinly, which would have dire consequences on the morning of April 2.

Heavy rain continued to fall during much of March 30. Lee held a meeting with his commanders on the right of his line, during which a courier arrived from Fitzhugh Lee stating that elements of Sheridan's cavalry conducting reconnaissance in strength had reached Five Forks and had driven in all of his pickets. Lee responded with a message giving his nephew command of the whole cavalry division, as Major-General Wade Hampton III had been sent south to assist Lieutenant-General Joseph Johnston's Army of the Tennessee in central North Carolina, and ordering him to attack the Union cavalry at Five Forks. He also ordered Pickett to extend his division towards Five Forks and then to attack the Union left flank by pushing down towards Dinwiddie Court House in

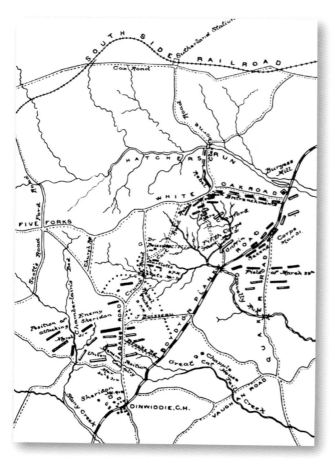

A map showing the whole area of action including Five Forks, White Oak Road, Boydton Plank Road and Dinwiddie Court House on March 31. One of the main objectives of the Union army, the Southside Railroad can be seen farther north. The position of Chamberlain's brigade across the White Oak Road by 5 p.m. that day is not shown. (*War Papers read before the State of Maine Commandery*)

conjunction with Anderson who would attack at his front, in order to flank Sheridan's cavalry. Pickett's Division took 18 hours to reach Five Forks enduring "the discomforts of rain, slush and hunger" as they marched. Having reached the intersection, Pickett decided after consultation with Fitzhugh Lee to throw out skirmishers, but not to advance on Dinwiddie Court House until the following morning.

Farther east, the Union II Corps continued its advance encountering abatis, or felled trees, but driving the Confederate pickets back into their hastily prepared main line of works consisting of logs and earth breastworks along the White Oak Road. By nightfall Humphreys had thrown up a temporary line of breastworks from the Crow House on Hatcher's Run to the intersection of the Dabney's Mill and Boydton Plank roads. The V Corps pushed north along the Quaker Road to its intersection with the Boydton Plank Road, and Ayres's 2nd Division was ordered towards the White Oak Road. Only picket skirmishing and exchange of artillery shots occurred during these maneuvers. During the night of the 30th Warren was ordered to move the divisions of Crawford (3rd) and Griffin (1st) within supporting distance of Ayres, whose position on the extreme left was considered likely to invite attack.

Dinwiddie Court House, March 31

The rain finally ceased about noon on March 31. At about 10 a.m. Pickett commenced his movement south from the White Oak Road towards Dinwiddie Court House. Marching down Scott's Road, he turned his infantry east to cross a swampy creek called Chamberlain's Bed at Danse's Ford, while two cavalry divisions under W.H.F. "Rooney" Lee, second eldest son of Robert E. Lee, and Thomas Rosser crossed about half a mile (800m) farther south at Fitzgerald's Ford. Alerted to this flanking movement by his scouts, Sheridan sent the cavalry brigades of Davies and Smith (2nd Division, Army of the Potomac) to cover the fords. Pickett's lead infantry brigades pushed Davies's troopers back, while the main thrust of Sheridan's cavalry consisting of the brigades of Stagg and Fitzhugh (1st Division) withdrew east from the Five Forks area after coming under pressure from Munford's Brigade of Virginia cavalry (Lee's Division). Sheridan ordered forward the brigades of Gibbs (1st Division) and Gregg (2nd Division) to attack Pickett's infantry in the rear, which stopped their march towards the left of the Union infantry and caused them to turn south towards the Court House. Soon after, Smith's brigade at Fitzgerald's Ford was pressed back by the cavalry of Lee and Rosser and was flanked by Pickett's infantry, which forced them to retire towards the Court House. Sheridan next ordered forward as reinforcements the brigades of Pennington and Capehart under Custer (3rd Division), plus four rifled cannon of Company A, 2nd US Artillery. As they arrived half a mile (800m) north of the Court House about 5.30 p.m., these forces began erecting low fence-rail breastworks behind which the troopers of Devin's repulsed 1st Division gathered.

Regarding this fight, several Northern newspapers later reported: "When Custer came to the front a scene of the wildest excitement prevailed … He instantly set Capehart's band to playing 'Hail Columbia' and other patriotic pieces. This revived the spirits of all present, and the music brought forth cheers from thousands of wearied men." As the combined Confederate cavalry and infantry force approached the Union defenses, Sheridan and Custer, with their staff officers, rode along the line with their respective colors displayed, which evoked further cheers from the ranks of the dismounted cavalrymen. Soon after, the rifled cannon of the regular artillery opened fire and, although they launched several assaults, the Confederates were unable to push Sheridan back into Dinwiddie Court House, and nightfall ended the action with the two forces laying on their arms not more than 100 yards (90m) apart. Although the Battle of Dinwiddie Court House was a tactical victory for the Confederates, they gained little strategically. Pickett had prevented Sheridan from reaching the Southside Railroad, but the Confederate infantry had at last been lured out of its siege lines and were now exposed to a flanking attack from the east from a far larger Union force.

White Oak Road, March 31

While Sheridan's cavalry fought Pickett's Division, Warren's V Corps engaged in battle with Johnson's Division (IV Corps) northeast of Dinwiddie Court House. If the White Oak Road could be seized, it would make it almost impossible for Anderson's Corps to support Pickett near Five Forks. Worst of all, Pickett's Division would be cut off from the main Confederate line. With Ayres's 2nd Division in advance in a wedge-like formation and without skirmishers, Crawford's 3rd Division in support, and Griffin's 1st Division as a reserve, the Union advance began about 10 a.m. on March 31 and pushed forward along a narrow woodland road, either side of which was swampy terrain broken by flooded ravines. Confederate skirmishers fired on the advancing infantry but fell back to their main works. Visiting with Anderson that morning, Robert E. Lee found the Federals at his immediate front at about 11 a.m., and quickly chose as an attack force the brigades of Moody and Wise of Johnson's Division, plus those of Hunton, who was detached from Pickett's Division (I Corps), and McGowan's brigade of Wilcox's Division (III Corps).

The small brigade commanded by Brigadier-General Joshua L. Chamberlain captured part of the White Oak Road on March 31, but were ordered to withdraw and march to the assistance of Sheridan's cavalry at Dinwiddie Court House. Chamberlain would later receive the formal surrender of the Confederate infantry on April 12. (Courtesy of the Appomattox Court House National Historical Park)

According to Ayres, his troops arrived within about 50 yards (45m) of the White Oak Road and began to throw up breastworks when the enemy's lines of battle, consisting of only four brigades, rose up in the woods and moved forward across the road into the open, driving back the 5,000-strong Federal division. Advancing at the double-quick along the left flank of Ayres's troops, McGowan's South Carolinians caught the Marylanders of Stanton's 2nd Brigade in a heavy enfilading fire, following which Ayres's infantry broke and ran, pushing through the ranks of Crawford's 3rd Division which was still forming its battle lines. Crawford's troops were also flanked and almost cut off. In his report of the action, Colonel John A. Kellogg stated that his 1st Brigade (3rd Division) was "somewhat broken up, owing to the fact that the enemy was in their rear, compelling them to fight their way back." Seeing Ayres's and Crawford's troops reeling back in disorder, Griffin ordered Joseph J. Bartlett's 3rd Brigade to throw up a breastwork on a rise in the ground behind which the retreating Union infantry rallied. As a result, Johnson's momentum was halted.

With the failure of this initial attack, Meade ordered Humphreys to send II Corps troops to support Warren's V Corps; as a result, two brigades of Miles's 1st Division launched a second, more successful assault by attacking the Confederate left flank while Chamberlain's small 1st Brigade of Griffin's 1st Division (V Corps) advanced on its front. With the weight of numbers, the Union infantry forced Lee to pull his troops back behind their breastworks following which Chamberlain's brigade captured a section of the White Oak Road line. In his account of the action Chamberlain wrote: "Now, quick or never! On and over! The impetuous 185th New York rolls over the enemy's right, and seems to swallow it up; the 198th Pennsylvania, with its fourteen companies, half veterans, half soldiers … swing in upon their left striking [Brigadier-General Eppa] Hunton's Brigade in front; and for a few minutes there is a seething wave of countercurrents … and all is over. We pour over the works; on across the White Oak Road; swing to the right and drive the enemy into their entrenchments along the Claiborne road, and then establish ourselves across the road facing northeast, and take breath." With his right flank "refused," or bent back at right angles so as to face westerly, Lee lost his direct link with Pickett's troops around Five Forks.

Instead of following up this success and launching a larger flanking attack on the Claiborne Road, Grant wished to take advantage of Pickett's isolation, and directed Warren to withdraw and send troops from his corps along the Boydton Plank Road during the night of March 31/April 1 in hopes of cutting off Pickett's infantry and cavalry before they withdrew from Dinwiddie Court House. However, due to difficulties crossing the flooded main branch of Gravelly Run, those sent, which consisted of Ayres's and Griffin's divisions, were held up and did not arrive until just before daybreak.

Meanwhile, learning from captured Union videttes that Union infantry was approaching his rear and left flank, Pickett realized he had no choice but to fall back. He wanted to reform his line along the north bank of Hatcher's Run, but Lee insisted that he should withdraw only as far as the crossroads known as Five Forks, which consisted of the intersection of the White Oak Road, Scott's Road, Ford's (or Church) Road, and the Dinwiddie Court House Road. Pickett did not like the flat terrain around Five Forks, which he believed to be indefensible. Nonetheless, Lee's telegram to Pickett stated: "Hold Five Forks at all hazards. Protect road to Ford's Depot and prevent Union forces from striking the Southside Railroad. Regret exceedingly your forced withdrawal [from Dinwiddie Court House], and your inability to hold the advantage you had gained."

Not present when Sheridan attacked at Five Forks, Major-General George E. Pickett was attending a fish bake with Thomas L. Rosser and rushed back to the White Oak Road line too late to influence the outcome of the battle. (Library of Congress LC-USZ6-284)

Five Forks, April 1

During the early hours of April 1, Pickett's Division waited behind a log and dirt breastwork which stretched about 1.75 miles (2.8km) along the northern side of the White Oak Road. Munford's cavalry (Lee's Division) was posted on the Confederate left flank at the intersection of the Gravelly Run Church and White Oak roads. Entrenched in the 150 yard (137m)-long angle, or "return," which also protected the left flank, was Ransom's North Carolinian Brigade (Johnson's Division, IV Corps). Close by were four guns of McGregor's Battery (Chew's Battalion). West of Ransom waited Wallace's South Carolinian Brigade (Johnson's Division), while the Virginians of Pickett's Division manned the rifle-pits and breastworks as far as Five Forks. Placed across Ford's (or Church) Road were three guns of Pegram's Battalion (Walker's Artillery, III Corps). To the left of the Forks lay Terry's Virginian brigade (Gordon's Division, I Corps), by then under Colonel Joseph Mayo, 3rd Virginia, as Terry had been disabled when his horse was killed. Next to this were three more of Pegram's guns and Corse's Brigade of Virginians (Pickett's Division). Holding the right flank, or western end, of the Confederate line were two brigades of "Rooney" Lee's cavalry.

Presumably taking advantage of "the lull before the storm," Pickett and Lee rode north of Hatcher's Run to enjoy a fish bake with Thomas Rosser, and did not inform the other officers in the line where they were going. They also failed to place someone in command in their absence. Also, due to atmospheric conditions known as an "acoustic shadow" which prevented them from hearing the sounds of battle, they were unaware of the fighting until it was too late.

Sheridan's plan of attack was to drive in the Confederate pickets and pin down the main Confederate line with his cavalry, now under Major-General Wesley Merritt as he was with the infantry, while Warren's V Corps would launch an attack on Pickett's left flank. No Union artillery was involved. As the ground in front of the Confederate position was too wet and swampy for mounted operations, the cavalry troopers were dismounted to attack on foot. Mackenzie's Cavalry Division (XXV Corps, Army of the James) was sent riding north of Dinwiddie Court House with orders to turn east and secure part of the White Oak Road to prevent Anderson from sending Pickett reinforcements. According to Mackenzie's report, this was achieved after "a sharp skirmish" during which two companies of the 11th Pennsylvania successfully charged and captured a Confederate breastwork and dispersed its occupants, who were greater in number than their assailants. Leaving a battalion of the 5th Pennsylvania to guard the Union right flank, Mackenzie rode west to join the main assault.

Published later in *Harper's Weekly*, this engraving depicts Sheridan leading the charge of Ayres's division, V Corps, on the Confederate left flank at Five Forks on April 1. (Author's collection)

As he waited for Warren to get his infantry into position, Sheridan received a dispatch from Grant. The lieutenant-general was disappointed with Warren's performance at White Oak Road on March 31, believing that his attack would have succeeded had he sent all three divisions forward rather than holding one in reserve. He also thought that Warren should have acted more quickly to prevent Pickett from falling back from the Dinwiddie Court House to consolidate his position along the White Oak Road. Thus, Grant stated that if in his judgment V Corps would do better under one of its division commanders, Sheridan was authorized to relieve Warren and order him to report to headquarters. Unaware of this development, Warren assembled his troops in line of battle either side of the Gravelly Run Church about 1,300 yards (1.2km) from the enemy left flank and obliquely to the White Oak Road, in order that the right of his battle line would strike the enemy as soon as possible after the center and left. On the east side of the church was Crawford's 3rd Division, while opposite and a little behind was Ayres's 2nd Division. Griffin's 1st Division was formed behind and to the right of Crawford. They were under orders to advance north along the Gravelly Run Road en echelon and upon reaching the intersection with the White Oak Road were to wheel left and attack the entrenched Confederates at "the angle."

Following the breakthrough on the Confederate left flank, the infantry of Crawford's 3rd Division, Warren's V Corps, attacks Pickett's line along the White Oak Road, and Corse's Virginia Brigade makes a last stand during the closing stages at Five Forks. According to the notes on this drawing by Alfred R. Waud, the rebels surrendered and massed around the tree depicted in the rear left. (Library of Congress LC-DIG-ppmsca-21363)

Finally ready to launch the assault by about 4 p.m., Warren's corps advanced and marched briskly forward across the miry bottomland that bordered Gravelly Run, through the undergrowth on the hillside beyond, and quickly reached an open level plain. Beyond this they saw the White Oak Road about 200 yards (180m) ahead. At this point they were joined by Mackenzie who was ordered to lead his small mounted brigade around to the right of the infantry and gain possession of the Ford Road leading from Five Forks across Hatcher's Run, thereby cutting off any possibility of Confederate retreat north.

Meanwhile, due to faulty reconnaissance and inaccurate maps Sheridan did not strike the eastern end of the Confederate line when he reached the White Oak Road. In fact, "the angle" at the end of the enemy position was 1,300 yards (1.2km) farther west, which seriously disrupted his plans. As a result, his two leading divisions began to lose contact as Ayres's troops, with Sheridan, wheeled left and progressed along the road while Crawford swung northwest, passing through woods beyond the Confederate line. Being ordered to provide support, Griffin's division followed Crawford; however, realizing his error, Griffin readjusted to fill the gap between the other two divisions. Fatefully, Warren rode off with an escort to find Crawford and get him back in the fight leaving Sheridan to lead the attack on "the angle."

Painted by French artist Paul Dominique Philippoteaux, who produced the Gettysburg Cyclorama, this battle scene depicts the Union cavalry charging the right wing of Pickett's Division during the Battle of Five Forks on April 1. (Virginia Historical Society accession number 2006.190)

Finally approaching the Confederate entrenchments through thick woodland, Ayres's 2nd Division opened fire at about 4.30 p.m.; this was immediately echoed along the White Oak Road by the carbines of Merritt's troopers, who responded to the preconcerted signal for assault and started forward.

Sheridan personally led the charge that breached "the angle." Holding that position, the 24th North Carolina bore the full impact of the assault and fell back on the other regiments of Ransom's Brigade. As his flank came under attack, Ransom sent a courier asking for reinforcements, but in Pickett's absence none of the other brigade commanders would take the responsibility for weakening the Confederate right. Thomas R. Roulac, a 1st Lieutenant of Company D, 49th North Carolina, later recalled: "The remainder of our line was hotly engaged with two lines of battle in their front, which had driven in our pickets, and advanced to the attack ... Running over the Twenty-fourth and Twenty-fifth [North Carolina], and driving the Fifty-sixth from their flank and rear, the enemy was upon us." Wallace's South Carolina Brigade (Johnson's Division), plus the 38th Virginia of Steuart's Brigade (Pickett's Division), attempted to form a new "return" perpendicular to the main trench line to hold back Warren's advance, but to no avail. After fierce resistance they also fell back in confusion towards Ford's Road and Five Forks.

Although his division fought well during the campaign leading up to and during the Battle of Five Forks, Major-General Gouverneur K. Warren was relieved from command by Sheridan under instructions from Grant for not acting decisively and committing all three divisions at White Oak Road the day before. (Library of Congress LC-DIG-cwpb-05647

Being finally alerted to the desperate situation on his left flank, Pickett galloped down Ford's Road to the Forks, and narrowly missed being shot as the skirmishers of Crawford's 3rd Division emerged from the woods to his right, having swung back around the rear of the White Oak Road line and thus almost encircling the Confederates. Attempting to seize control of the situation, Pickett ordered Terry's/Mayo's brigade to form a line across Ford's Road in an effort to stop Crawford. It was also urged to assist Steuart. But Crawford's infantry smashed through Terry's/Mayo's

Virginians scattering or capturing most of them. Continuing along the line in conjunction with Ayres, the combined Union divisions encountered yet another hastily formed "return" near the Gilliam House as Corse's Brigade (Pickett's Division) made a last-ditch effort to hold their ground. As the sun was setting, what remained of Pickett's Division was finally beaten and began to surrender or make their escape along a narrow woodland road to their rear. In the closing stages of the battle, George C. Custer sent two of his 3rd Division cavalry brigades around the Confederate right in order to cut off this escape route; however, they encountered strong resistance from some infantry plus "Rooney" Lee's cavalry, which enabled most of the surviving Southerners on the extreme right flank to get away.

At his headquarters near Dabney's Mill, Grant received word of his victory at about 9 p.m. Apprehensive that Lee might evacuate the Petersburg trenches during the night and attack Sheridan before support troops could reach him, he made the monumental decision to order a bombardment along the entire Petersburg line; this commenced about 9 p.m. following which a general assault was to begin. The Union victory at Five Forks was overshadowed by Warren's removal from command. Although the V Corps commander's advance had been slowed by muddy conditions, tangled undergrowth and inaccurate maps, Sheridan blamed him personally for the delay and confusion which ensued during the earlier part of the battle, and during the events of the day before. Warren was replaced by Brigadier-General Charles Griffin, and resigned his commission as major-general in protest on May 27, 1865, reverting to his permanent rank as major in the Corps of Engineers. His numerous requests for a court of enquiry to clear his name were refused until Grant retired from the presidency in 1877, following which President Rutherford B. Hayes ordered a court of inquiry that convened in 1879 and found that Sheridan's removal of Warren had been unjustified. Unfortunately, this decision was not published until after Warren's death in 1882.

Captured at Five Forks on April 1, Confederate prisoners line up to be marched to the rear. A Federal officer recalled: "Droves of silent 'Johnnies,' under guard, tramped through the mire, jostling against noisy 'Yanks,' who were filling the air with yells and cat-calls – the effervescence of victory." (Library of Congress LC-DIG-cwp-02581)

The Confederate defeat at Five Forks was the breaking point for the Army of Northern Virginia. Lee had lost in killed, wounded, captured and stragglers at least 7,000 men in the battles from March 30 to April 1. The Southside Railroad, one of the last lifelines keeping Petersburg and Richmond supplied with food and war materiel, was now within the grasp of Grant's army. At his headquarters in the Turnbull House at Edge Hill on the Cox Road, about a mile west of Petersburg, Lee received the first report of Five Forks during the afternoon of April 1 and realized he must reinforce the right of his line. From east to west, he had only 11,000 men in the trenches from the Appomattox River to Hatcher's Run. From Lieutenant's Run, where the works became less formidable, to the very end of his fortified position, where the Claiborne Road crossed the western stretch of Hatcher's Run, he had no more than 12,500 infantry. These included troops in the highly important position of Burgess Mill, which defended the northern end of the Boydton Plank Road. On average, the Confederate infantrymen in these trenches were posted 10ft (3m) apart. In some places the gap between each man was even greater.

To properly re-man these endangered works, Lee next ordered Field's Division (I Corps) of 4,600 men from the north side of the James, and directed that Longstreet accompany them. In what was possibly going to be his last campaign, Lee wanted his most able lieutenant by his side. As Field's departure would leave only Kershaw's Division of infantry, Gary's Brigade of cavalry (Lee's Division) and some heavy artillery north of the James, the alarm was sounded in the capital and all the local defense troops, plus the Virginia Military Institute cadets, were ordered out under Ewell to man the works south of Richmond. The safety of the troops on the extreme right of the Confederate line was now dependent on how quickly Field's Division could reach Petersburg and be deployed in the line before a major Union assault began. Progress, however, was slow aboard the railroad cars that carried the division south.

Union breakthrough, April 2

The mass Union assault on Petersburg began at about 4.30 a.m. on April 2. Parke's IX Corps advanced on the line centering on Fort Mahone (Battery 29), also known as "Fort Damnation," to the east of Petersburg but was met with stiff resistance from Grimes's Division of Gordon's II Corps. Axe-carrying infantrymen spearheaded the attack as they hacked their way through abatis and chevaux-de-frise. By 6.50 a.m., Parke had captured two forts, two redans and 12 guns, but the Confederates tenaciously held on to their inner line of defenses known as the Dimmock Line after Colonel of Ordnance Charles H. Dimmock, who supervised their construction.

At 4.40 a.m., a signal gun at Fort Fisher announced the attack of Wright's VI Corps on the Confederate lines defending the Boydton Plank Road. Getty's 2nd Division spearheaded the attack. Echeloned on its left was Seymour's 3rd Division while Wheaton's 1st Division followed on the right. Advancing in a "wedge-shape" formation with axemen clearing the way, they swept back the enemy pickets and quickly reached the main Confederate trenches. Confronting them was Lane's North Carolina Brigade of Wilcox's Division (III Corps). Following 20 minutes of desperate hand-to-hand fighting, the Union infantry finally broke through the siege lines and virtually cut in half Lee's army defending Petersburg. Of this action, Brigadier-General James H. Lane recalled: "my line was pierced by the enemy in strong force at the ravine in front of the right of the Thirty seventh [North Carolina] near General [Samuel] McGowan's headquarters. The Twenty eighth [North Carolina], enfiladed on the left by this force, and on the right by the force that had previously broken the troops to our right, was forced to fall back to the Plank road. The enemy on its left took possession of this road and forced it to fall back still further to the Cox road." Regrouping after their breakthrough, most of VI Corps turned southwest inside the Confederate lines and attacked the rest of Ambrose P. Hill's infantry holding the line on the north bank of Hatcher's Run.

Other elements of VI Corps turned east after reaching the Boydton Plank Road and attacked Thomas's Georgia Brigade of Wilcox's Division, which widened the breach in the Confederate line even further. Joined by remnants of Lane's Brigade, the Georgians fell back towards forts Gregg and Whitworth, two earthworks on the western end of the Petersburg defenses, while others scrambled into the inner defensive Dimmock Line, which ran from batteries 45 to 55 about 1,300 yards (1.2km) behind the forts.

Farther west, Humphreys's II Corps began their assault by 6 a.m. on the Crow House redoubt located near Hatcher's Run just north of Dabney's steam sawmill. Capturing it within two hours, they continued their advance occupying the Confederate trench line running from Burgess Mill to the Claiborne Road which had already been abandoned as its defenders had fallen back upon Sutherland's Station. The II Corps divisions commanded by Hays (2nd) and Mott (3rd) were next ordered eastward along the Boydton Plank Road towards Petersburg to link up with VI Corps.

Meanwhile at Lee's headquarters at the Turnbull House on the western end of the inner Petersburg line, Longstreet had arrived ahead of Field's Division at about 1 a.m. and attempted to sleep on the floor of the adjutant's office. Concerned about the increasing noise of battle along the lines, Ambrose P. Hill joined the exhausted but sleepless Lee at about 5.15 a.m., having just returned to the army from sick leave the day before. Shortly after this, aide-de-camp Colonel C.S. Venable observed wagons and teamsters driving wildly through the mist along the Cox Road towards Petersburg. Investigating further, Venable recalled: "Walking out on the road, I met a wounded officer on crutches coming from the direction of the huts of Harris's brigade [Mahone's Division], which lay across the branch in front of the headquarters, who informed me he had been driven from his quarters in these huts (which a few sick and wounded men occupied) by the enemy's skirmishers. I immediately returned to the house, ordered my horse, and reported what I had seen and heard to General Lee, with whom General Hill was still sitting. General Lee ordered me to go and reconnoitre at once." Desperate to find out what had happened in his sector of the line, Hill rode off with Venable only to be shot through the heart by a Union infantryman several minutes later. Thus Lee lost one of his most able lieutenants, and the third-highest-ranking general in his army. His III Corps was hereafter combined with I Corps under Longstreet.

By about 10 a.m., the advanced brigade of Miles's 1st Division had reached the Cox Road at Sutherland's Station and found three Confederate brigades under Cooke holding breastworks and trenches about a half mile in length, behind which ran the Southside Railroad. Placed in position by Heth, who then returned to Petersburg, the Southern defenders consisted of the mixed brigades of MacRae and Cooke (of Heth's Division) and McGowan and Scales (of Wilcox's Division). The first Union attack was thrown back with heavy casualties including 3rd Brigade's commander Henry J. Madill, who was severely wounded and was replaced by Brigadier-General Clinton D. MacDougall. After two further assaults, the last main pocket of resistance in the outer Petersburg defenses had fallen by about 3 p.m. on April 2, and the Southside Railroad was at last severed.

In the meantime, still at his headquarters at the Turnbull House, Lee observed a battle line of Federal troops advancing towards him and was informed by Longstreet that Field's Division had still not arrived in Petersburg. With his army now cut in two and his last supply line severed, Lee's only choice was to rally the remaining Confederate forces at his disposal on forts Gregg and Whitworth, and withdraw any troops south of those forts to the inner defences, which consisted of low earthworks in the suburbs of the city. He now made the fateful decision to abandon Petersburg, which inevitably meant also evacuating Richmond. He determined to withdraw his troops from the whole front as soon as darkness fell, and to concentrate what remained of them, as previously planned, at Amelia Court House near the Richmond & Danville Railroad, which provided a vital link with the south and Johnston's Army of the Tennessee in North Carolina. Thus he dictated to Colonel Walter H. Taylor, his chief aide-de-camp, a telegram for the Secretary of War. Reviewing the facts, it outlined his plan and concluded: "I see no prospect of doing more than holding our position till night. I am not certain that I can do that. If I can I shall withdraw to-night north of the Appomattox, and if possible, it will be better to withdraw the whole line tonight from James River. The brigades on Hatcher's Run are cut off from us; enemy have broken through our lines and intercepted between us and them ... I advise that all preparation be made for leaving Richmond tonight. I will advise you later, according to circumstances." In turn, Taylor dictated the message to the telegram operator, who sent it directly to the War Department in Richmond. It was received at 10.40 a.m. on April 2 and was then carried to President Jefferson Davis, who was attending morning service in Saint Paul's Episcopal Church, Richmond. Davis read it, got up quietly, and left the building.

Forts Gregg and Whitworth, April 2
In order to affect a successful withdrawal from Petersburg and the Confederate capital, Lee needed time for Field's Division to cross from the north side of the James to man the inner defenses. The defenders of Fort Gregg and, to a lesser extent, Fort Whitworth would provide him with the respite needed. The two fortified batteries defended the line just to the west of a ravine defined by Rohoic (or Old Town) Creek, less than 4 miles (6km) from the center of Petersburg. Standing about 250 yards (230m) in the rear of the main trench line, Fort Gregg was a five-sided lunette earthwork with provision for guns protected by a deep, water-filled ditch approximately 14ft wide and 8ft deep (4.2 x 2.4m), with a zigzag wooden palisade and sally port guarding its rear. Since August 1864, this post had been manned by approximately 75–80 artillerymen detached from Hill's III Corps and serving as infantry under the immediate command of 1st Lieutenant Frank McElroy, 3rd Company, Washington Artillery.

About 700 yards (640m) north of Fort Gregg stood Fort Whitworth, also known as Fort Alexander by the Confederates, and Fort Baldwin by the Federals, which was originally a fully enclosed earthwork consisting of a seven-sided redoubt. By April 1865 this was described as "an indefensible work … washed-out … and not over knee high." Despite these deficiencies, Fort Whitworth contained four rifled Parrott guns.

An unfinished trench and embankment projecting about 30 yards (27m) from its northwest corner towards Fort Whitworth created a weakness in the defenses of Fort Gregg, making it easier for an attacker to climb to the top of the wall. Unfortunately this had escaped the notice of every Confederate officer associated with this sector of the defenses.

A quarter of a mile (400m) southeast of Fort Gregg on the main trench line was a newly completed earthwork called Fort Owen, after Lieutenant-Colonel William Miller Owen, who had responsibility for all the works in the vicinity. Owen had commanded the Battalion Washington Artillery until the summer of 1864 and on March 25, 1865 was placed in command of McIntosh's Artillery Battalion of Wilcox's Division. A section of the 1st Company, Washington Artillery under 1st Lieutenant Henry A. Battles, manned two 3-inch rifle cannon in this post.

Shortly after the Confederate line was broken, McElroy opened musketry fire on the skirmishers of the 2nd Brigade, 1st Division, Wright's VI Corps, led by Colonel Joseph E. Hamblin, as they approached from the southwest. Later McElroy recalled: "There being no artillery in the fort, and my ammunition reduced to one thousand rounds, and no prospects of receiving more, I was compelled to slacken my fire." This indicates that at this point the Confederate defenders had only about 16 rounds apiece. This would be supplemented by a further 1,000 rounds before the main Union attack began.

Meanwhile, 1st Lieutenant Battles and his gun crews in Fort Owen were overrun and captured, and artillerists among the Union troops commenced loading one of the rifled guns as they turned it on Fort Gregg. After sending a detail to bring up some horses, McElroy concentrated his musket fire on the threatening gun and forced the enemy to temporarily abandon the fort, following which he led a detachment and reoccupied the battery. Receiving the horses, McElroy ordered the guns dragged to a ridge just east of the Banks House, from which vantage point he could see great numbers of the enemy in three or four lines of battle advancing east inside the Confederate lines. Readying his guns, he fired 35 rounds from each piece, following which Owen ordered him back to Fort Gregg, where he placed the guns inside the works.

Entitled "The 24th Corps charging a fort to the left," this sketch by Alfred R. Waud depicts the defense of Fort Gregg by just 334 Confederates on April 2. Based on the artist's pencil notation, Colonel James C. Briscoe, 199th Pennsylvania, is the officer to the right of the flag shown urging his regiment on. Seen at left, Fort Whitworth is shown rather too close to Fort Gregg than it actually was. This action held up the Union advance sufficiently to allow Lee to deploy Field's Division along the Petersburg inner line for the purpose of covering the withdrawal of the Army of Northern Virginia that night. (Library of Congress LC-USZ62-12803)

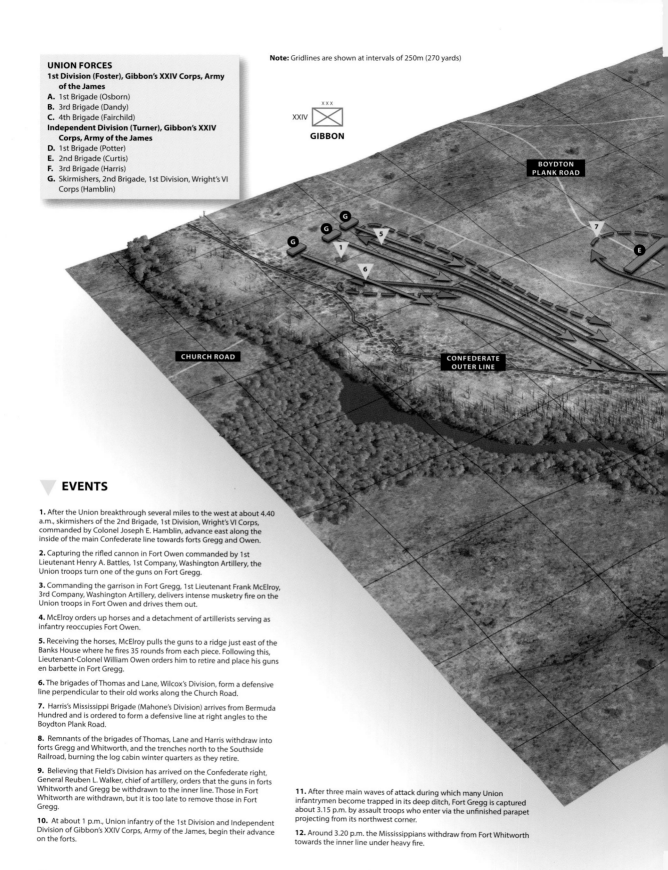

Note: Gridlines are shown at intervals of 250m (270 yards)

UNION FORCES

1st Division (Foster), Gibbon's XXIV Corps, Army of the James
- **A.** 1st Brigade (Osborn)
- **B.** 3rd Brigade (Dandy)
- **C.** 4th Brigade (Fairchild)

Independent Division (Turner), Gibbon's XXIV Corps, Army of the James
- **D.** 1st Brigade (Potter)
- **E.** 2nd Brigade (Curtis)
- **F.** 3rd Brigade (Harris)
- **G.** Skirmishers, 2nd Brigade, 1st Division, Wright's VI Corps (Hamblin)

XXIV

GIBBON

BOYDTON PLANK ROAD

CHURCH ROAD

CONFEDERATE OUTER LINE

▼ EVENTS

1. After the Union breakthrough several miles to the west at about 4.40 a.m., skirmishers of the 2nd Brigade, 1st Division, Wright's VI Corps, commanded by Colonel Joseph E. Hamblin, advance east along the inside of the main Confederate line towards forts Gregg and Owen.

2. Capturing the rifled cannon in Fort Owen commanded by 1st Lieutenant Henry A. Battles, 1st Company, Washington Artillery, the Union troops turn one of the guns on Fort Gregg.

3. Commanding the garrison in Fort Gregg, 1st Lieutenant Frank McElroy, 3rd Company, Washington Artillery, delivers intense musketry fire on the Union troops in Fort Owen and drives them out.

4. McElroy orders up horses and a detachment of artillerists serving as infantry reoccupies Fort Owen.

5. Receiving the horses, McElroy pulls the guns to a ridge just east of the Banks House where he fires 35 rounds from each piece. Following this, Lieutenant-Colonel William Owen orders him to retire and place his guns en barbette in Fort Gregg.

6. The brigades of Thomas and Lane, Wilcox's Division, form a defensive line perpendicular to their old works along the Church Road.

7. Harris's Mississippi Brigade (Mahone's Division) arrives from Bermuda Hundred and is ordered to form a defensive line at right angles to the Boydton Plank Road.

8. Remnants of the brigades of Thomas, Lane and Harris withdraw into forts Gregg and Whitworth, and the trenches north to the Southside Railroad, burning the log cabin winter quarters as they retire.

9. Believing that Field's Division has arrived on the Confederate right, General Reuben L. Walker, chief of artillery, orders that the guns in forts Whitworth and Gregg be withdrawn to the inner line. Those in Fort Whitworth are withdrawn, but it is too late to remove those in Fort Gregg.

10. At about 1 p.m., Union infantry of the 1st Division and Independent Division of Gibbon's XXIV Corps, Army of the James, begin their advance on the forts.

11. After three main waves of attack during which many Union infantrymen become trapped in its deep ditch, Fort Gregg is captured about 3.15 p.m. by assault troops who enter via the unfinished parapet projecting from its northwest corner.

12. Around 3.20 p.m. the Mississippians withdraw from Fort Whitworth towards the inner line under heavy fire.

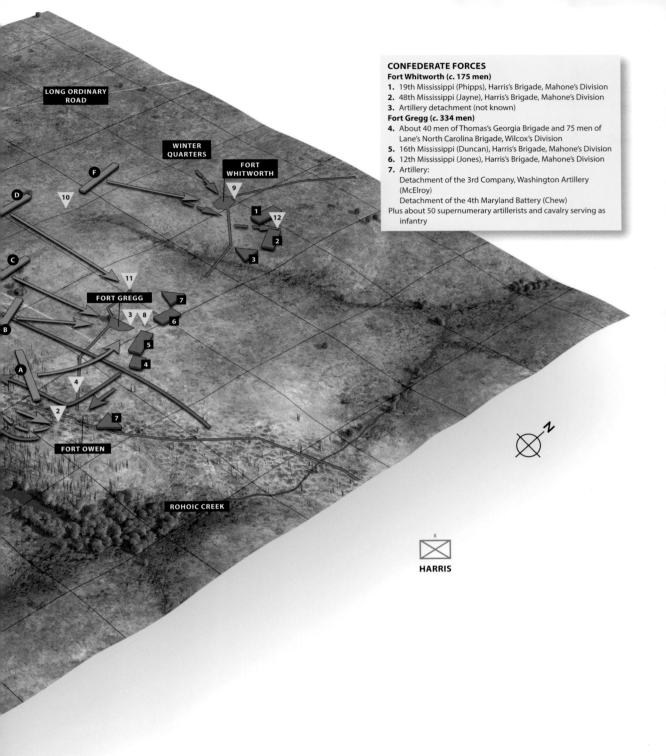

CONFEDERATE FORCES

Fort Whitworth (c. 175 men)
1. 19th Mississippi (Phipps), Harris's Brigade, Mahone's Division
2. 48th Mississippi (Jayne), Harris's Brigade, Mahone's Division
3. Artillery detachment (not known)

Fort Gregg (c. 334 men)
4. About 40 men of Thomas's Georgia Brigade and 75 men of Lane's North Carolina Brigade, Wilcox's Division
5. 16th Mississippi (Duncan), Harris's Brigade, Mahone's Division
6. 12th Mississippi (Jones), Harris's Brigade, Mahone's Division
7. Artillery:
   Detachment of the 3rd Company, Washington Artillery (McElroy)
   Detachment of the 4th Maryland Battery (Chew)

Plus about 50 supernumerary artillerists and cavalry serving as infantry

LONG ORDINARY ROAD

WINTER QUARTERS

FORT WHITWORTH

FORT GREGG

FORT OWEN

ROHOIC CREEK

HARRIS

ASSAULT ON FORTS GREGG AND WHITWORTH, APRIL 2, 1865

The defense of forts Gregg and Whitworth buys Lee time to conduct a successful withdrawal from Petersburg and the Confederate capital. However, an unfinished parapet projecting from Gregg's northwest corner provides an opportunity for the Union attackers.

At his headquarters at the nearby Gregg House, Major-General Cadmus Wilcox received word that Harris's Mississippi Brigade, of Mahone's Division (III Corps), was approaching at the double quick having been ordered from the Howlett Line trenches on Bermuda Hundred at midnight on April 1. In the meantime, Wilcox ordered the remains of the brigades of Thomas and Lane of his division to counterattack by forming a battle line perpendicular to their old works. Advancing towards the Federals, they reoccupied some of the trenches from which they had been driven earlier that morning. As the North Carolinians and Georgians reached the Church Road, Harris's Mississippi Brigade arrived in support and was ordered to assist in delaying the Union advance as long as possible.

Harris next led the 19th and 48th Mississippi into Fort Whitworth and the trenches from that point north to the Southside Railroad, while Captain James H. Duncan took a detachment of about 150 men from the 12th and 16th Mississippi into Fort Gregg. About 40 men from Thomas's Georgia Brigade under Captain William Norwood, and 75 of Lane's North Carolina Brigade led by Lieutenant George H. Snow, 33rd North Carolina, also entered the fort. Manning the two cannon inside was a mixed command of artillerymen composed of the Louisianans under McElroy who worked the gun at the southeast corner embrasure, and those commanded by Captain Walter Chew, 4th Maryland Battery, who fired the gun in the center embrasure. Together with about 50 infantrymen, or artillerists serving as infantry, the number of Confederates in Fort Gregg amounted to approximately 330. As those with muskets were deployed along the firing step, and gun crews loaded their pieces with canister, General Wilcox addressed them through the noise of battle: "Men, the salvation of Lee's army is in your keeping; you must realize the responsibility, and your duty; don't surrender this fort; if you can hold the enemy in check for two hours Longstreet [meaning Field's Division, I Corps], who is making a forced march, will be here, and the danger to the army in the trenches will be averted."

As the massed Union infantry approached, Wilcox returned to the Gregg House where he learned that Brigadier-General Reuben L. Walker, chief of artillery (III Corps), had bypassed his authority and sent a confusing dispatch to both forts ordering the guns withdrawn to the inner line before they fell into Union hands. Walker later claimed that he issued this order based on the news that Field's Division had arrived on the Confederate right. As a result, and under protest, the four guns in Fort Whitworth were pulled out leaving its defense to the Mississippi infantry under Harris, but the enemy was too close to permit the removal of the two guns in Fort Gregg. The withdrawal of the artillery from Fort Whitworth was a turning point in the battle. As Wilcox later explained, "The guns in these two batteries had the widest possible field of fire, they being in barbette [able to fire over the parapet] the mutual support and protection designed by the engineers for these two works to give the one to the other was thwarted at the critical moment ... the four guns – had they remained – could have delivered a rapid fire of schrapnel [sic] and grape upon the flank of the enemy, scarcely four hundred yards distant. It is probable, had this been done, the enemy would have been repulsed, and although Gregg would have been finally captured, yet during the time of preparation for a renewal of the assault the little garrison might have been withdrawn." Unfortunately for the Confederates, as soon as the Federals realized that artillery fire from Fort Whitworth had ceased, they increased the ferocity of their attack.

Amounting to about 5,000 men, the Union infantry consisting of Foster's 1st Division and Turner's Independent Division (Gibbon's XXIV Corps, Army of the James) began its advance at about 1 p.m. As Rohoic Creek had been flooded by a dam constructed by Confederate engineers to create a wide barrier of water which ran south of the forts, Gibbon's troops had to approach from the southwest. Foster's division formed the right wing with Dandy's 3rd and Osborn's 1st brigades in the first wave of attack. In echelon to their rear left was Fairchild's 4th Brigade. The brigades of Curtis (2nd) and Potter (1st) of Turner's Independent Division formed the next assault wave, while Harris's 3rd Brigade of this division advanced through the log-cabin winter quarters burned by the retreating Confederates and attacked Fort Whitworth. Three attempts were thrown back, but with the fourth charge (about 2.30 p.m.) the Union troops finally forced their way into Fort Gregg.

On two occasions, Union troops managed to fight their way through the gated stockade in the rear of the fort but were thrown back by a bayonet charge. As each wave of attack was repulsed, many men remained out of sight in the ditch. Commanding remnants of the 16th Mississippi inside the fort, Captain Archibald K. Jones observed that when the assailants "got in twenty-five or thirty yards of the fort they were safe, for we could not see them again until they appeared upon the parapet." Of the moment the 10th Connecticut reached the ditch, Chaplain Trumball recorded: "Men jumped into the breast-high water, and making a living bridge of each other, clambered up the steep sides beyond." The Mississippian Jones further commented: "I am satisfied that the last assaulting column walked on the heads of the other columns, who were packed in the ditch like sardines in a box, for they made no halt at all, but rushed right on over the parapet into the fort." In fact, most of those who finally entered the fort climbed up the unfinished parapet that projected towards Fort Whitworth.

As the weight of sheer numbers carried them forward, Union flags appeared along the parapet like "a solid line of bunting," according to Jones. Running out of ammunition, the Confederates resorted to throwing stones and bricks at their assailants, and Captain Leach heard them shouting to each other "Never surrender! Never surrender!" As the Federals began to swarm over the parapet in front of the right-hand gun nearest the stockade, a Union officer demanded that 18-year-old driver Laurent Biri, alias Bery or Berry, of the 3rd Company, Washington Artillery, should surrender. The only member of the gun crew still not wounded or dead, Biri shouted back defiantly "Pull and be damned," as he yanked the lanyard and blasted canister through all in front of him. Seconds later Biri was also shot dead. The loss to the defenders of Fort Gregg was 57 killed, 129 wounded and 30 captured, while the total killed and wounded sustained by Gibbon's XXIV Corps was 714 men. After the surrender, many of the Union infantry were so elated that they discharged their muskets in the air; this led the Confederates to their left to believe that prisoners-of-war were being given no quarter, and for a short time they shelled the fort.

As Fort Gregg fell, Harris's 3rd Brigade of Turner's division advanced on Fort Whitworth through the smoke of the burning winter quarters and the Mississippians remained at their post until the enemy was within 40 yards (36m) of them, when an aide arrived from Wilcox ordering them to fall back to the inner line. As they retired under heavy fire, about 85 men were captured including Colonel Joseph M. Jayne, 48th Mississippi, who was one of several wounded. The brave defense of Fort Gregg, and to a lesser extent Fort Whitworth, allowed Field's division to reinforce the inner line and to throw up breastworks where a gap of about 1 mile (1.6km) existed between the end of the Dimmock Line and the Appomattox River. The determined stand at Fort Gregg would also give Lee the time he needed to evacuate the remains of his army from the Petersburg defenses.

In the Union ranks, Birney's 2nd Division of XXV Corps next arrived and occupied the captured Confederate trenches facing Lee's newly fortified inner line. With the flooded banks of Rohoic Creek at their front and the Confederates on higher ground on the opposite side, Ord decided against pressing the attack in this sector any further. Meanwhile, southeast of Petersburg Parke's IX Corps had less success although it did capture some Confederate earthworks near the Jerusalem Plank Road. Although an attempt about 11 a.m. by Grimes's Division of Gordon's II Corps to retake several captured batteries was pushed back, Parke sent an urgent telegraph message to Meade requesting reinforcements. In response Meade sent Seymour's 3rd Division (VI Corps). During another Confederate advance begun at approximately 1 p.m., Brigadier-General Robert B. Potter was wounded and replaced in command of the 2nd Division (IX Corps) by Simon G. Griffin. The last of Gordon's counterattacks took place around 3 p.m.; although it pushed back the Federals around Fort Mahone, it was stopped by the arrival of Collis's Independent Brigade from the City Point defenses. Shortly after this, Gordon received orders to begin the evacuation of what remained of his corps back into Petersburg in preparation for a general withdrawal.

After VI Corps mopped up pockets of Confederate resistance as far southwest as Hatcher's Run, its two remaining divisions marched along the Boydton Plank Road towards Petersburg, and then veered north on the Long Ordinary Road towards Lee's headquarters at Edge Hill. This important post was defended by the artillery of Poague's Battalion, which opened fire with canister. As they formed in line of battle, some of the Union infantrymen later claimed they saw Lee riding away from the Turnbull House to the safety of the Dimmock Line. Having been under arms for over 18 hours, Wright's corps was too exhausted for another assault and began erecting breastworks opposite the inner Confederate line.

Farther west at Five Forks, Sheridan's cavalry and V Corps, now under the command of Charles Griffin, saw little action. After crossing the Southside Railroad in the afternoon, Griffin marched east along the Cox Road towards the sound of battle but, learning that Miles's 1st Division had overcome Confederate resistance at Sutherland's Station, he next moved to the junction of the Namozine and River roads where he went into bivouac.

Also heading north from Five Forks, Sheridan's troopers pursued the retreating Confederates. Following their defeat, remnants of the commands of Pickett, Johnson and Fitzhugh Lee had gathered at Church Road Crossing on the Southside Railroad. The next day they continued north towards the Appomattox River, which they hoped to ford at Exeter Mills. Serving as a rearguard, W.H.F. Lee's troopers discovered around 3 p.m. that Sheridan's cavalry was approaching, following which Johnson's infantry threw up breastworks across the Namozine Road at Scott's Cross Roads. Several hours later, elements of Devin's cavalry division approached and made several unsuccessful attempts to dislodge Johnson's troops, but darkness ended the action. Meanwhile, Pickett had proceeded to Exeter Mills only to find the Appomattox River too deep to ford. Using a ferry boat to cross some of Ransom's Brigade, he decided it would take too long to transfer his whole

Union breakthrough on the Petersburg line, April 2, 1865.

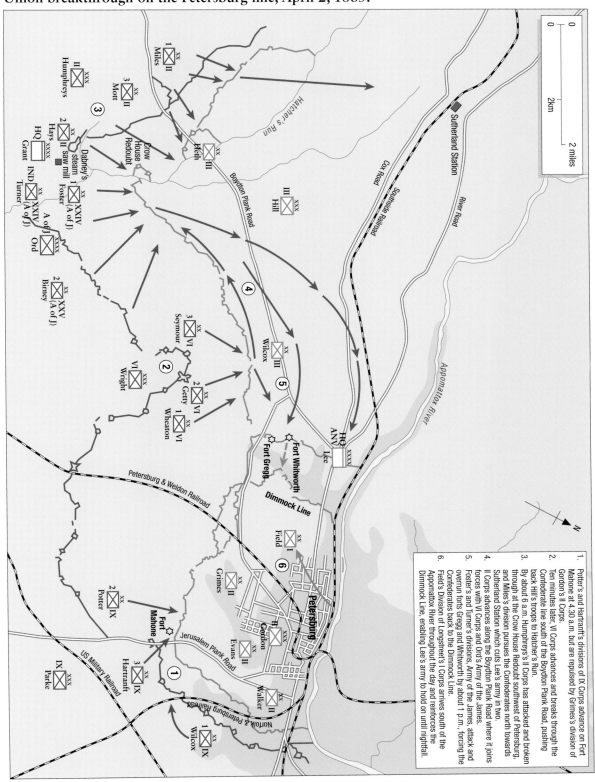

1. Potter's and Hartranft's divisions of IX Corps advance on Fort Mahone at 4.30 a.m. but are repulsed by Grime's division of Gordon's II Corps.

2. Ten minutes later, VI Corps advances and breaks through the Confederate line south of the Boydton Plank Road, pushing back Hill's troops to Hatcher's Run.

3. By about 6 a.m. Humphreys's II Corps has attacked and broken through at the Crow House Redoubt southwest of Petersburg, and Miles's division pursues the Confederates north towards Sutherland Station which cuts Lee's army in two.

4. II Corps advances along the Boydton Plank Road where it joins forces with VI Corps and Ord's Army of the James.

5. Foster's and Turner's divisions, Army of the James, attack and overrun forts Gregg and Whitworth by about 1 p.m., forcing the Confederates back to the Dimmock Line.

6. Field's Division of Longstreet's I Corps arrives south of the Appomattox River throughout the day and reinforces the Dimmock Line, enabling Lee's army to hold on until nightfall.

command by this means and moved northwest, eventually joining the forces of Fitzhugh Lee, "Rooney" Lee, and Bushrod Johnson in crossing Deep Creek on April 3, 1865.

CONFEDERATE WITHDRAWAL FROM PETERSBURG AND RICHMOND, APRIL 2–3

After his retreat to the inner defenses, Lee established a temporary headquarters at the McIlwaine House in Petersburg. During the early evening of April 2 he sent his last message to the War Department in Richmond, stating: "It is absolutely necessary that we abandon our position tonight, or run the risk of being cut off in the morning." At 8 p.m., and under cover of darkness, the remains of the Army of Northern Virginia began to evacuate their lines around Petersburg and Richmond. The artillery was quietly moved out first, followed by the infantry minus pickets, who would finally withdraw from their posts at 3 a.m. Meanwhile, President Davis and his cabinet had left the Confederate capital via the Richmond & Danville Railroad by 11 p.m. heading for Danville, just north of the North Carolina border, where they could stay in contact with the armies of both Lee and Johnston.

Various routes for the withdrawal of troops had been planned in advance by Colonel Thomas Talcott, commander of the Confederate Engineer Corps. The immediate point of destination was Amelia Court House on the Richmond & Danville Railroad which was 39 miles (63km) southwest of Richmond and 36 miles (58km) northwest of Petersburg. In order to ensure his army could reach that point, Lee had to affect a successful crossing of the Appomattox River. During the winter of 1864/65 he had ordered Engineer troops to rebuild Bevils road bridge over the river about 25 miles (40km) above Petersburg, which had been partially destroyed by Confederate troops in June 1864. This was the most direct route to Amelia Court House. Another pontoon bridge was ready for use at the site of Goode's road bridge over the Appomattox. Finally, on April 2 the reserve pontoon train in Richmond was sent to Mattoax Station via the Richmond & Danville line, from which point it was to be transported overland about 2 miles (3.2km) farther north to the site of the Genito road bridge to provide a river crossing at that point for the wagon trains.

With the exception of Bushrod Johnson's infantry and Fitzhugh Lee's cavalry which headed west along the Namozine and Tabernacle roads, the army at Petersburg slipped out of the trenches they had occupied for ten months and crossed to the north side of the Appomattox River via four bridges. At the eastern end of the city, Gordon's II Corps used

Photographed by Timothy O'Sullivan during the following month, this view of the Appomattox River running through Petersburg shows the Campbell Bridge and the road ascending in the background towards Ettrick's cotton mill along which the troops to the west of the city escaped during the Confederate withdrawal on April 2–3. (Library of Congress LC-DIG-ppmsca-35599)

the Pocahontas and Richmond & Petersburg Railroad bridges, and headed off along the Hickory Road. Those to the west of the city center escaped via Campbell's Bridge, which crossed to Ettrick's cotton mill. Farther west, Lee and Longstreet crossed via a pontoon bridge near the Battersea Cotton Mill with the remains of Wilcox's, Heth's and Field's divisions, and took the River Road. About 1,000 wagons plus artillery not needed with the troops was taken via the Woodpecker Road towards Chesterfield Court House. Left behind was all the heavy artillery, which was spiked and disabled before departure. Once the bulk of the army was on the north bank of the river, Lee ordered his engineers to destroy the Pocahontas and Campbell bridges. The rear-guard comprising Field's troops burned the cotton warehouses in the city and destroyed the bridge at the Battersea factory and the pontoon bridges.

Commencing the evacuation of Richmond and its defenses at midnight on April 2, Ewell's Reserve Corps abandoned the capital by 7 a.m. the next day. Crossing the James River to Manchester over the Mayo Bridge, they marched along New Road to Branch's Church then passed by Tomahawk Baptist Church to the Genito Road hoping to reach Amelia Court House by crossing over the Appomattox via the pontoon bridge at Genito Mill. The main wagon train trundled towards Meadville near where it was to cross the Appomattox at Giles Bridge.

South of Richmond, the troops in the lines near Chaffin's Bluff under George Washington Custis Lee, the commanding general's eldest son, and mainly composed of heavy artillerymen, crossed the James River via the pontoon bridge to Drewry's Bluff. There they were joined by the Naval Brigade under Commodore J. Randolph Tucker, composed of about 400 to 600 Confederate States Navy personnel who had manned the batteries at Drewry's Bluff, plus approximately 200 Marines under Captain John D. Simms from Camp Beall. Marching west via Chesterfield Court House, this combined force of soldiers, seamen and marines fell in with Ewell's column at Tomahawk Church. Farther south at Bermuda Hundred, elements of Mahone's Division (III Corps) withdrew towards Chester and then moved on to Chesterfield Court House, after which they made their way to the pontoon bridge at Goode's Bridge. En route they were joined by the troops under Longstreet and Gordon.

Abandoning the lines near Fort Gilmer, Kershaw's Division (I Corps) marched up the New Market Road into Richmond. Before arriving at the Mayo Bridge, Kershaw was ordered to detach two battalions to suppress the mob sacking the city. The last Confederate troops to leave

This detail from a stereograph shows the flooded Appomattox River; it delayed Lee's retreat and caused him to divert his Petersburg column north from the Bevils Bridge crossing to Goode's Bridge, which was already congested by Mahone's troops. (Library of Congress LC-DIG-cwpb-02782)

Pursuit of Lee's retreat to Amelia Court House and beyond, April 2–3, 1865.

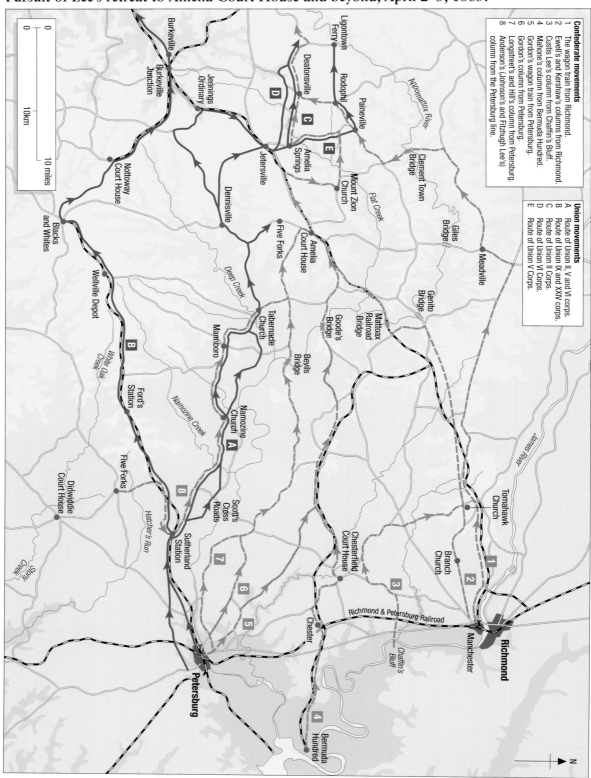

Confederate movements
1 The wagon train from Richmond.
2 Ewell's and Kershaw's columns from Richmond.
3 Custis Lee's column from Chaffin's Bluff.
4 Mahone's column from Bermuda Hundred.
5 Gordon's wagon train from Petersburg.
6 Gordon's column from Petersburg.
7 Longstreet's and Hill's column from Petersburg.
8 Anderson's, Johnson's and Fitzhugh Lee's) column from the Petersburg line.

Union movements
A Route of Union II, V and VI corps.
B Route of Union IX and XXIV corps.
C Route of Union II Corps.
D Route of Union VI Corps.
E Route of Union V Corps.

Richmond were the mounted cavalrymen of Gary's Brigade (Lee's Division), who crossed the James River via Mayo's Bridge, all other bridges by this time having been destroyed, and then escorted the wagon train towards Meadville. Behind them burned the warehouses filled with tobacco, put to the torch by Confederate Provost-Marshal Major Isaac N. Carrington.

After a march of about 12 miles (19km), Kershaw's troops fell in behind those of Ewell and G.W.C. Lee and continued along the Genito Road, also in hope of negotiating the Appomattox River via a pontoon bridge at Genito Mill. Learning on April 4 that the Confederate Engineer Bureau had failed to ship the pontoon train from Mattoax Station to the Genito Bridge, the whole column of troops from the Richmond area was forced to march several miles farther south to the railroad crossing at Mattoax. Furthermore, Lee and Longstreet learned from scouts that due to spring flooding the approaches to Bevils Bridge were impassable; this forced them farther north to cross via Goode's Bridge, which was already congested by Mahone's column. Thus, although Lee's plans counted on three available road route crossings of the Appomattox for troops, artillery and wagon trains, only two bridges were available and one of them was the Richmond & Danville railroad bridge at Mattoax Station, which had a difficult approach and crossing for wheeled vehicles.

UNION OCCUPATION AND PURSUIT, APRIL 3

During the early hours of April 3, Union troops began to enter Petersburg and Richmond. East of Petersburg Lieutenant-Colonel Ralph Ely's 2nd Brigade (1st Division, IX Corps) passed through the deserted Confederate lines about 3.10 a.m. Seeing the clock tower of the courthouse in the distance, the 1st Michigan Sharpshooters and 2nd Michigan Infantry raced into the city. Reaching the courthouse first, a member of the former regiment, Color Sergeant William T. Wixsey, scrambled up into the tower and, opening the glass of the clock face, thrust out his regimental colors at 4.28 a.m. Wixsey later recalled: "Our hearts were too full of utterance, so we clasped our hands and shed tears of joy, for we knew that the beginning of the end had come." This was the first US flag flown over Petersburg for about four years. The 2nd Michigan raised their flag over the Customs House shortly after.

South and west of Petersburg elements of Brigadier-General John Hartranft's 3rd Division (IX Corps) advanced to the city limits by about 4.15 a.m. and were joined by Hamblin's 2nd Brigade (1st Division, VI Corps), which encountered city mayor William W. Townes plus a member of the Common Council carrying a white flag of truce. Led

As they occupy Petersburg, Union troops march past the burned-out workshops, water towers and wrecked cars at the Southside Railroad Depot in this pencil and Chinese white drawing by Alfred Waud. (Library of Congress LC-USZ62-14292)

In this detail from a glass stereograph, a few curious citizens watch as a Union supply train enters Petersburg after the collapse of the Confederate defenses on April 2. (Library of Congress LC-DIG-cwpb-01286)

to Colonel Oliver Edwards, commanding 3rd Brigade, 1st Division of VI Corps, Townes officially surrendered the city and handed over the following note: "The city of Petersburg having been evacuated by the Confederate troops, we, a committee authorized by the Common Council, do hereby surrender the city to U.S. forces, with a request for the protection of the persons and property of its inhabitants." At Bermuda Hundred, Major-General George Hartsuff's Union infantry division advanced on the Howlett Line to find it evacuated. On April 4, his troops were ordered to assume control of Petersburg, City Point and the surrounding area.

Outside Richmond, Major-General Godfrey Weitzel, commanding the Army of the James in Ord's absence, sent a cavalry detachment of about 40 men of the 4th Massachusetts Cavalry (Provost Guard, XXV Corps) under majors Atherston H. Stevens and E.E. Graves along the Osborne Turnpike to receive the surrender of the city. About 3 miles (5km) south of Richmond at about 5.30 a.m. they met Mayor Joseph Mayo and his committee riding in an open carriage. Mayo handed Stevens a similar note to that received at Petersburg requesting that an organized Union force take possession of the city "to preserve order and protect women and children and property." Accepting the surrender document, Stevens and his party continued into Richmond riding into Capitol Square at about 7 a.m. There they dismounted and raised two cavalry guidons over the statehouse, the first Union colors to fly over the city after its fall. Meanwhile, Major-General Weitzel marched his African-American troops into Richmond, and going directly to the City Hall received the formal surrender at 8.15 a.m. on April 3.

Back at Petersburg, Major-General George Meade rode into the city at about 8 a.m. and found Grant at the house of lawyer Thomas Wallace on Market Street who, according to a reporter, "was suddenly transformed into a Union man by the magic influence of triumphant bayonets." Lincoln also entered the city and congratulated Grant on his success shortly after. Discussing the situation, his two generals, Grant and Meade, attempted to work out Lee's possible strategy and agreed that the Confederate commander would retreat along the Richmond & Danville Railroad into North Carolina. To stop him linking up with Johnston's Army of the Tennessee, Grant determined to cut off his avenue of escape by marching for Burkeville Junction, the point at which the Southside and Richmond & Danville railroads crossed. The actual route taken by most of Lee's army via Amelia Court House to Burkeville was approximately 55 miles (88km), while Grant's intended route from Sutherland's Station along the Namozine Road was only about 35 miles (56km). Thus, the Union forces would have a 20-mile (32km) advantage, provided all went according to plan. Before leaving Petersburg for Sutherland's Station, Grant sent a dispatch to Sheridan

A cavalry escort leads the carriages of Confederate officials fleeing across Mayo's Bridge over the James River during the night of April 2. Charged with guarding the bridge until the last troops had crossed, Captain Clement Sulivane recalled: "the waters sparkled and dashed and rushed on by the burning city. Every now and then, as a magazine exploded, a column of white smoke rose up as high as the eye could reach, instantaneously followed by a deafening sound." (Courtesy of the Anne S.K. Brown Military Collection)

instructing him that the "first object of [the] present movement will be to intercept Lee's army, and the second to secure Burkeville." The II, V and VI Corps would be tasked with the former action, while the IX and XXIV Corps would ensure that Lee's escape route along the railroad was cut.

Parke's IX Corps would also guard wagon trains and picket the Southside Railroad in rear of the main army. Transportation of supplies, and the evacuation of casualties, was essential to the success of Grant's campaign and to ultimate victory, and some of these troops were detailed to realign the rails on the Southside from the wider 5ft gauge to that of the US Military Railroad, which had the standard northern gauge of 4ft 8½ in. Eventually, IX Corps was spread along the railroad from Sutherland's Station to Farmville and as a result was not actively engaged in the remainder of the Appomattox Campaign, although it performed a vital role.

This engraving based on a sketch by W.L. Sheppard shows the citizens of Richmond seeking refuge in Capitol Square during the conflagration following the evacuation of the Confederate government. Looters can be seen setting fire to property while the Capitol Building stands in the background. (*Battles & Leaders*)

Action at Namozine Church, April 3

Although the Confederate withdrawal from Petersburg and Richmond went reasonably well, the Confederate troops still south of the Appomattox River had to fight their way to Amelia Court House. Following the skirmish with Sheridan's cavalry at Scott's Cross Roads on April 2, the column under Bushrod Johnson and Fitzhugh Lee continued westward along the Namozine Road with Lee's troopers acting as rearguard. Reaching the 50ft (15m)-wide Namozine Creek by 2 a.m. the next day, they received news that the Petersburg and Richmond lines had been broken, and were ordered to withdraw to Amelia Court House. With elements of Custer's 3rd Division in pursuit,

Escaping with much of his command after Five Forks, Major-General Bushrod R. Johnson led his infantry towards Amelia Court House on the south side of the Appomattox River and fought Custer's cavalry during the rearguard action at Namozine Creek on April 3. (Library of Congress LC-USZ62-71561)

Bushrod Johnson placed William P. Roberts's small brigade, consisting of the cavalry of the 4th North Carolina and 16th North Carolina Battalion (W.H.F. Lee's Division), behind breastworks on the west bank of the creek with Wise's Brigade of Virginia infantry (Johnson's Division, IV Corps) farther upstream to their right. According to a Northern newspaper correspondent accompanying Custer's command, the Confederates also felled trees across the ford to impede pursuit.

Appearing on the opposite bank at daybreak, Custer ordered Battery A, 2nd US Artillery, to open fire with canister. Of this action Brigadier-General Henry Wise recalled: "Sheridan's cavalry sounded the bugle notes of charge … from a heavy wood in our front. This was but a feint to deceive Fitzhugh Lee's dismounted cavalry on our left." While the cannon fire kept the North Carolinians occupied, the 1st Vermont Cavalry (Wells's Brigade, Custer's 3rd Division) was dismounted and crossed further down stream to attack the right flank of Roberts's troopers. According to Wise: "the enemy pressed decidedly upon [Roberts], when he called for reinforcements from the infantry. We ordered the 59th [Virginia] down the breast-works immediately, leaped them before reaching the cavalry, formed at right angles … on the enemy's left, and scattered them at the first volley."

Having held up the Union pursuit as long as they could, the Confederates withdrew towards Namozine Church and Wintercomac Creek about 5 miles (8km) distant. Meanwhile, Custer's cavalry removed the obstructions, forded the creek without further resistance and continued the pursuit with the brigade of Colonel William Wells fighting a running battle with Roberts's troopers. Of this part of the action Sheridan reported to Grant: "The resistance made by the enemy's rear guard was very feeble. The enemy threw their artillery ammunition on the sides of the road and into the woods and then set fire to the fences and woods through which the shells were strewn."

When the Confederates reached Namozine Church they divided forces with "Rooney" Lee's cavalry and Bushrod Johnson's infantry striking out along Green's Road towards the Bevils Bridge Road while the rest of the cavalry under Fitzhugh Lee and Rosser continued along the Namozine Road. Meanwhile, rearguard duty at Namozine Church was taken over by the 800-man strong North Carolina brigade of Brigadier-General Rufus Barringer ("Rooney" Lee's Division). According to Barringer, the 5th North Carolina Cavalry was dismounted and concealed near the church in "some out-buildings and along an old fence row with a view to a possible surprise [i.e. ambush]," while the 1st and 2nd North Carolina Cavalry, with a single gun of McGregor's Virginia Horse Artillery, stood mounted behind makeshift breastworks facing east at the intersections of the Green's, Namozine and Cousin's roads. Guarding the wagon train, the 3rd North Carolina Cavalry was not involved in the ensuing action.

The 8th New York Cavalry, of Wells's Brigade, was the first of Custer's units to approach the Confederate line about 9 a.m. Probing briefly, they fell back, where they were joined by the 1st Vermont Cavalry; both regiments attacked, with the 8th New York wheeling around towards the enemy's right flank. Observing this, Barringer ordered the 2nd North Carolina to charge but his counterattack failed and the 1st North Carolina was successfully outflanked and thrown into confusion. With the arrival of a third Union regiment, the 15th New York Cavalry (Wells's Brigade), the mounted Confederate troopers broke and either fell back or surrendered.

With the 5th North Carolina in danger of being cut off and captured, Barringer sent orders for them to remount and retire along Green's Road. Years later he recalled: "But all in vain; in less than thirty minutes my mounted lines were overwhelmed with numbers, and the Fifth Regiment exposed to certain capture. Orders for this regiment to retire had all been miscarried or been unheeded, when I myself, as a last resort, dashed across the field, with two of my staff, to guide them in person through a heavy wood (still unoccupied by the enemy). This saved the dismounted men, though their horses were lost." In the confusion, Barringer and several of his staff became separated from the main body and fell in with what he thought was a Confederate cavalry escort; this group led them towards the Appomattox River along Namozine Road, and then captured them at pistol point, declaring they were Sheridan's scouts wearing Confederate uniforms. Barringer thus concluded: "in my efforts to rejoin the division, I was deceived … and was myself so captured." The total Confederate loss at Namozine Church amounted to 350 men killed, wounded or captured plus 100 horses and one cannon taken. Also, the battle flag of the 2nd North Carolina was captured by the commanding general's brother – Lieutenant Thomas W. Custer, Company B, 6th Michigan Cavalry, Stagg's Brigade, Devin's 1st Division – for which he received the Medal of Honor. But despite his losses, Barringer had bought enough time for "Rooney" Lee and Johnson to discover that the bridge over Deep Creek at the Green's Road crossing was impassable. As a result they marched south to join Fitzhugh Lee, who had arrived at the small settlement of Mannboro on the Cralle Road leading to Brown's Bridge over Deep Creek, which it was still possible to cross.

Meanwhile, Custer ordered his 3rd Brigade under Colonel Capehart to pursue the Confederate column along Green's Road while Wells's 2nd Brigade was dispatched along the Namozine Road and caught up with Johnson's infantry at Mannboro. Although the Confederate brigades of Moody, Wallace and Wise (Johnson's Division) were formed in line of battle, they were driven back about 2 miles (3km) to Sweathouse Creek where the Federals halted their pursuit, allowing Johnson to cross over Deep Creek, pass by Tabernacle Methodist Church and rest in the vicinity of the Bevils Bridge Road intersection. That night they were joined by that part of Pickett's Division which had failed to cross the Appomattox at Exeter Mills.

Photographed on January 4, 1865, George Armstrong Custer commanded the 3rd Division, Cavalry Corps, Army of the Shenandoah, fought at Five Forks, Namozine Church, Little Sailor's Creek and Appomattox Station, and played a decisive role in the final day at Appomattox Court House. (Library of Congress LC-B813-1613 A)

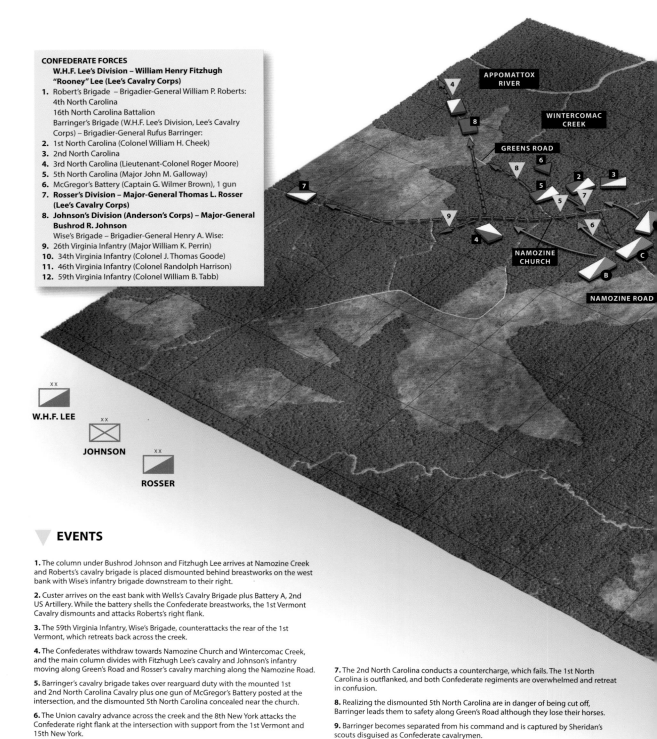

CONFEDERATE FORCES

W.H.F. Lee's Division – William Henry Fitzhugh "Rooney" Lee (Lee's Cavalry Corps)

1. Robert's Brigade – Brigadier-General William P. Roberts:
   4th North Carolina
   16th North Carolina Battalion
   Barringer's Brigade (W.H.F. Lee's Division, Lee's Cavalry Corps) – Brigadier-General Rufus Barringer:
2. 1st North Carolina (Colonel William H. Cheek)
3. 2nd North Carolina
4. 3rd North Carolina (Lieutenant-Colonel Roger Moore)
5. 5th North Carolina (Major John M. Galloway)
6. McGregor's Battery (Captain G. Wilmer Brown), 1 gun
7. **Rosser's Division – Major-General Thomas L. Rosser (Lee's Cavalry Corps)**
8. **Johnson's Division (Anderson's Corps) – Major-General Bushrod R. Johnson**
   Wise's Brigade – Brigadier-General Henry A. Wise:
9. 26th Virginia Infantry (Major William K. Perrin)
10. 34th Virginia Infantry (Colonel J. Thomas Goode)
11. 46th Virginia Infantry (Colonel Randolph Harrison)
12. 59th Virginia Infantry (Colonel William B. Tabb)

APPOMATTOX RIVER

WINTERCOMAC CREEK

GREENS ROAD

NAMOZINE CHURCH

NAMOZINE ROAD

W.H.F. LEE

JOHNSON

ROSSER

▼ EVENTS

1. The column under Bushrod Johnson and Fitzhugh Lee arrives at Namozine Creek and Roberts's cavalry brigade is placed dismounted behind breastworks on the west bank with Wise's infantry brigade downstream to their right.

2. Custer arrives on the east bank with Wells's Cavalry Brigade plus Battery A, 2nd US Artillery. While the battery shells the Confederate breastworks, the 1st Vermont Cavalry dismounts and attacks Roberts's right flank.

3. The 59th Virginia Infantry, Wise's Brigade, counterattacks the rear of the 1st Vermont, which retreats back across the creek.

4. The Confederates withdraw towards Namozine Church and Wintercomac Creek, and the main column divides with Fitzhugh Lee's cavalry and Johnson's infantry moving along Green's Road and Rosser's cavalry marching along the Namozine Road.

5. Barringer's cavalry brigade takes over rearguard duty with the mounted 1st and 2nd North Carolina Cavalry plus one gun of McGregor's Battery posted at the intersection, and the dismounted 5th North Carolina concealed near the church.

6. The Union cavalry advance across the creek and the 8th New York attacks the Confederate right flank at the intersection with support from the 1st Vermont and 15th New York.

7. The 2nd North Carolina conducts a countercharge, which fails. The 1st North Carolina is outflanked, and both Confederate regiments are overwhelmed and retreat in confusion.

8. Realizing the dismounted 5th North Carolina are in danger of being cut off, Barringer leads them to safety along Green's Road although they lose their horses.

9. Barringer becomes separated from his command and is captured by Sheridan's scouts disguised as Confederate cavalrymen.

BATTLE OF NAMOZINE CHURCH, APRIL 3, 1865

Despite a defeat with a loss of 350 captured including Colonel Rufus Barringer, the Confederate rearguard action at Namozine Creek and near Namozine Church delayed the Union pursuit sufficiently for "Rooney" Lee and Johnson to find an alternative crossing over Deep Creek after finding the Green's Road Bridge was impassable.

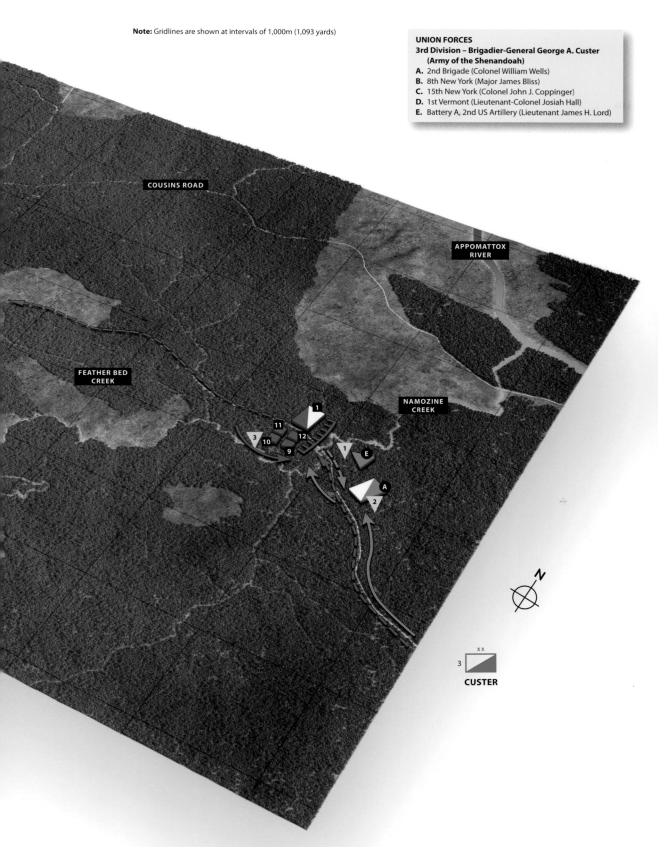

Note: Gridlines are shown at intervals of 1,000m (1,093 yards)

COUSINS ROAD

APPOMATTOX RIVER

FEATHER BED CREEK

NAMOZINE CREEK

N

XX
3 CUSTER

53

With his exhausted troopers also in need of rest, Custer went into bivouac along Sweathouse Creek, to be joined by Merritt and the troopers of Devin's 1st Division. Still accompanied by Sheridan, Griffin's V Corps infantry with the cavalrymen of Crook's 2nd Division marched past them as far as the Deep Creek crossing, where they also halted for the night. Coming along behind was Humphreys's II Corps followed by Wright's VI Corps. Most of the former went into camp near Wintercomac Creek, while the latter rested along the Namozine Road near Mount Hope Church. Progressing along the Cox Road farther south was Ord's Army of the James, which encamped about 3 miles (5km) west of Sutherland's Station. Leaving Wilcox's 1st Division to garrison Petersburg, the remainder of Parke's IX Corps hurried behind VI Corps, intent on reaching Burkeville before Lee. Thus, Grant and Meade had about 69,000 Federal troops in pursuit of Lee's dwindling army.

Commanding his brigade of North Carolina cavalry at Namozine Church, Brigadier-General Rufus Barringer was captured by Sheridan's scouts dressed in Confederate uniforms after helping many of his men to escape. (Courtesy of Jay Barringer and Kenneth W. Miller)

Amelia Court House, April 4

By dawn on April 4, Longstreet's column accompanied by Lee had completed its crossing of the Appomattox River via Goode's Bridge and proceeded toward Amelia Court House. After passing over the same bridge, Gordon's II Corps rested at Scott's Shop several miles west of the river. On arrival at the small county seat, Lee and his staff made for the Richmond & Danville Railroad station where they opened up waiting boxcars, expecting to find some of the 300,000 rations it was believed had been ordered sent from Richmond. Unfortunately, due to a breakdown in communication and mix-up in orders, these had not arrived, and in later years Isaac M. St. John, Chief of the Commissary Department, plus all of his assistants, denied ever receiving an order to send such rations. St. John further maintained that rations could easily have been sent as sufficient was held at the capital and the railroad to Amelia Court House was still operational.

As a result, Lee would have to rely on reserve rations in his wagon train plus whatever extra food could be found locally. Thus he issued a proclamation to the local populace: "I must therefore appeal to your generosity and charity to supply as far as each one is able the wants of the brave soldiers who have battled for your liberty for four years." He concluded by promising that the quartermaster department would pay for the food or supply "proper vouchers or certificates." He also ordered a message to be telegraphed from Jetersville requesting that 200,000 rations be brought up the railroad from Danville. Although he sent wagons out into the surrounding countryside to gather what food could be found, the local farmers had little to give and most of them returned practically empty. Lee also ordered Brigadier-General William N. Pendleton, commanding the Confederate reserve artillery, to reduce the number of guns following his columns. If possible these were to be sent by rail to Danville. Likewise, his chief quartermaster Colonel James L. Corley was required to slim down the number of wagons.

In the meantime the other Confederate columns continued to converge on Amelia Court House. Learning that Giles Bridge (near Meadville) was destroyed, the wagon train from Richmond eventually crossed the river over the Clement Town Bridge and headed towards Paineville, attempting to reunite with the army. Farther south, Mahone's progress was hindered as his rearguard had to delay destroying Goode's Bridge until they received word that the Richmond columns had crossed the Appomattox. Ewell, Kershaw and G.W.C. Lee finally managed to negotiate a crossing via the Mattoax railroad bridge by laying planks over the railroad tracks, thus affording a reasonably level surface to enable their wagons and artillery to reach the western bank after nightfall on April 4. These troops continued on to Amelia Court House during the early hours of April 5.

Although what remained of Lee's army was beginning to regroup, the breakdown in communication which had led to failure to send the much-needed rations to Amelia Court House, and the delay caused while Lee waited for the arrival of the columns from Richmond, plus those coming from south of the Appomattox River, was a major turning point in the Appomattox campaign as it lost a day's march for the Confederates and enabled the Federal troops to overtake them and cut off their escape route south.

Jetersville, April 4

By the beginning of April 4 it was becoming clear to the Federal commanders that Lee was concentrating his army at Amelia Court House with the intention of moving via Burkeville towards North Carolina as Grant had predicted. In order to block Lee's avenue of escape, the cavalry of Crook's 2nd Division was sent southwest towards Jenning's Ordinary, midway between Burke's Station and Jetersville on the Richmond & Danville Railroad. Once the railroad was reached, it was to move northeast along the tracks towards Jetersville. The remainder of the cavalry, with the V Corps following behind, marched through Dennisville and then turned directly towards Jetersville.

Crossing Deep Creek, the cavalry brigades of colonels Stagg (1st) and Fitzhugh (2nd) of Devin's 1st Division pressed forward to reconnoiter and encountered the Confederate rearguard cavalry of Fitzhugh Lee near Tabernacle Church. Pushing them back past Drummond's Mill and across Beaverpond Creek, they found elements of Heth's, Pickett's and Johnson's infantry in line of battle along Bevils Bridge Road at the intersection with Tabernacle Church Road at about 10 p.m., but withdrew after darkness had descended on April 4. The Confederate troops in this action finally began to reach Amelia Court House by dawn of April 5.

Further disaster struck Lee when Sheridan's advance guard arrived at Jetersville at about 5 p.m. on April 4. Entering the telegraph office, they intercepted the message about to be sent from the Confederate Commissary Department requesting 200,000 rations be dispatched by railroad from Danville to feed Lee's starving troops. As a result, Sheridan ordered a courier off to Burkeville to telegraph the message from there, in hope that the Confederate commissary at Danville might be deluded into sending the supplies into Union lines – but there is no evidence that this deception worked.

As the lead troops of the V Corps infantry began to arrive at Jetersville, they were ordered to throw up earthworks diagonally across the railroad. At this point if Lee had attacked, he might by sheer weight of numbers have pushed his way through and succeeded in reaching Burkeville before

ATTACK ON THE CONFEDERATE WAGON TRAIN AT PAINEVILLE, APRIL 5, 1865 (PP. 56–57)

Some of the infantry defending the main Confederate wagon train when it was attacked by the 1st New Jersey Cavalry (1), commanded by Colonel Hugh Janeway, were African-Americans (2) recently recruited in Richmond. An unknown Confederate officer who witnessed the action observed: "Several engineer officers were superintending the construction of a line of rude breastworks … Ten or twelve negroes were engaged in the task of pulling down a rail fence; as many more occupied in carrying the rails, one at a time, and several were busy throwing up the dirt … The [blacks] thus employed all wore good gray uniforms and I was informed that they belonged to the only company of colored troops in the Confederate service, having been enlisted in Richmond by Major [Thomas P.] Turner. Their muskets were stacked, and it was evident that they regarded their present employment in no very favorable light."

About the same time, while serving as a courier, Private R.M. Doswell of the Confederate Signal Corps saw "a wagon train guarded by … negro soldiers," and stated "[it was] a novel sight to me. When within about one hundred yards of and in the rear of the wagon train, I observed some Union cavalry a short distance away on elevated ground forming to charge and the negro soldiers forming to meet the attack, which was met successfully, the Union cavalry retreating they charged again, and the negro soldiers surrendered."

Supported by the 1st Pennsylvania Cavalry and 24th New York Cavalry, the Union troopers then rode along the train capturing prisoners and destroying wagons (3). Consumed in the burning wreckage at this point were 20,000 Confederate rations which would otherwise have sustained Lee's starving troops. Davies then turned back to Jetersville with his spoils which included 320 white, and 310 black, Confederate prisoners (the latter being referred to as only "teamsters"), 11 flags, 5 pieces of artillery, 180 wagons, and over 400 horses and mules. Having had his headquarters wagon destroyed, plus those of his cavalry corps, Fitzhugh Lee lamented, "Lost everything save what I have on … Desks, papers &c all burnt."

Parke's IX Corps could cut off his line of retreat. Lying in his path was only one division of cavalry and a single corps of infantry, with no other Union force within supporting distance. However, Lee was too disorganized and in no position to attack and, in the early hours of April 5, Sheridan sent couriers to Meade, who was ill with a cold and resting overnight near Deep Creek, urging him to "hurry on and reinforce him, lest Lee should escape." Meade responded immediately upon receiving this information. Although the troops were exhausted from marching, pushing wagons through mud and corduroying roads, and despite the fact they lacked rations as the supply wagons were still far in the rear, they were issued an "order of march" at 2 a.m. on April 5 and struggled on to reinforce Sheridan.

Paineville, April 5

When the Confederates failed to attack his position, Sheridan became suspicious that Lee might be attempting to take a circuitous route around Jetersville, and thus directed Crook to reconnoiter north of his position; this resulted in Davies's 1st Brigade of cavalry being sent out along the Amelia Springs Road. Arriving at the Paineville crossroads, scouts learned that the main Confederate wagon train from Richmond was approaching from the direction of Union Court House, and Davies immediately ordered his 1st New Jersey Cavalry, commanded by Colonel Hugh Janeway, to attack it. Accompanying the column with remnants of the 12th Virginia Cavalry, Sergeant William H. Arehart recorded in his diary: "about 10 o'clock A.M. the enemy attacked our wagon train." Having accompanied the reserve ordnance wagons from Bermuda Hundred to Amelia Court House, Confederate Lieutenant Frederick Colston rode on towards Paineville to overtake the Richmond train, and at about 10 a.m. found "a great state of confusion and disorder" as the Union cavalry made its approach.

Although this young African-American in Confederate uniform was possibly a "body servant" taken to war by a wealthy Southerner, he might equally represent the type of youngster recruited into military service during the closing stages of the war and who fought against Union cavalry near Paineville on April 5. (Courtesy of Bill Elswick)

In his official report of the action, Union Major Walter R. Robbins, 1st New Jersey Cavalry, stated: "Pushing rapidly on we soon struck the [Confederate] advance guard [and] at once charged and routed this force;" they also prevented it from bringing a cannon to bear on the Federal troopers. Davies next sent the 1st Pennsylvania Cavalry and 24th New York Cavalry riding along the length of the train, capturing prisoners and taking animals while destroying the wagons belonging to Fitzhugh Lee's cavalry corps.

Receiving news that his main supply train was under attack, Lee ordered "Rooney" Lee's cavalry division after Davies, while the small brigade under South Carolinian Martin Gary (Lee's Division) also closed in on the retreating Federals. As a result, Janeway found Confederate troops in his rear as he attempted to recross the bridge during his withdrawal towards Paineville to rejoin Davies's command. A charge conducted by two of his companies forced a passage across the creek and a rearguard action continued as the prisoners and captured property was driven south. According to Major Robbins's official report: "The enemy here displayed a much larger force than our own – they lapped both our flanks and engaged us sharply in our front; but the regiment ... used their Spencer carbines with telling effect."

The Confederate cavalry continued to pursue Davies's brigade to within a mile (1.6km) of Jetersville where a fierce mounted mêlée occurred in which 30 Union troopers were killed and 150 wounded, "principally with the saber," according to Fitzhugh Lee. With Union reinforcements approaching, the Confederate cavalry fell back towards Amelia Springs, where they encamped on the north bank of Flat Creek. Regarding the aftermath of this action, Confederate Lieutenant Frederick Colston commented: "We reorganized the train and resumed our march, and moved all night, passing through Deatonsville."

Meanwhile, Sheridan continued to consolidate his position at Jetersville. Humphreys's troops began to arrive there accompanied by Meade between 2.30 and 3.00 p.m. Still unwell and traveling in an ambulance, the commander of the Army of the Potomac requested that the infantry continue to be formed in an entrenched line of battle, and II Corps was placed on the left of V Corps. The VI Corps started to arrive at about 6 p.m. and was ordered to the right of the line. By nightfall on April 5, three Union army corps were dug in along a 4-mile (6.5km) front facing northeast towards Amelia Court House with Custer's cavalry guarding the flank.

Still progressing along the Southside Railroad, Ord's column was accompanied by Grant while Gibbon's XXIV Corps pushed on to reach Burkeville Junction, which they did late that evening, having marched 52 miles (83km) since leaving the trenches at Petersburg and 28 miles (45km) that day. As he rode towards Burkeville, Grant and his small entourage encountered a Federal scout at about 6.30 p.m. who delivered a dispatch from Sheridan informing him of Davies's successful attack on the main Confederate wagon train earlier that day. The cavalry commander ended his message thus: "I wish you were here yourself. I feel confident of capturing the Army of Northern Virginia if we exert ourselves. I see no escape for Lee." Receiving a fresh mount, Grant and escort immediately rode 20 miles (32km) across country to Jetersville finally arriving there about 10.30 p.m. Assessing that orders already issued by the ailing Meade would have permitted Lee to escape, he directed that all three army corps should advance on Amelia Court House during the early hours of the next morning, advising that "it was not the aim only to follow the enemy, but to get ahead of him," and adding that he had no doubt Lee was "moving right then." As a result, the troops advanced at dawn with V Corps moving along the Danville railroad, II Corps to its left and VI Corps to its right. At the same time Sheridan's cavalry was ordered in the direction of Deatonsville, 5 miles (8km) west of the railroad, while Ord was directed to cut the railroad bridge, known as High Bridge, which crossed the Appomattox River near Farmville.

In this sketch by Alfred R. Waud of the action near Paineville in Amelia County on April 5, elements of what were possibly Black Confederate infantry are shown raising their muskets as a sign of surrender as the 1st New Jersey Cavalry charges towards the wagon train they were protecting. (Library of Congress LC-DIG-ppmsca-21448)

High Bridge, April 6

Grant was correct in his assumption. The Army of Northern Virginia had already begun its march southwest from Amelia Court House towards Burkeville with the cavalry leading the way. Longstreet's I Corps headed the main column, behind which came Mahone's Division (III Corps), followed by Anderson's command and the divisions of Pickett and Johnson. Meanwhile, Ewell was just arriving at the Court House with the divisions of Kershaw (I Corps) and G.W.C. Lee. Before the column had progressed very far, Confederate scouts ran into Sheridan's dismounted cavalry skirmishers, beyond which was the V Corps infantry, and "Rooney" Lee galloped back along the files of trudging Confederate infantry to inform generals Lee and Longstreet. Debating whether to battle a way through, or seek an alternative route, Lee decided on the latter and turned his column west along the road towards Mount Zion Church.

Based on eyewitness accounts from Union infantrymen in the Petersburg trenches, this engraving based on a sketch by Theodore R. Davis showing two African-Americans in Confederate uniform was published in *Harper's Weekly* on January 10, 1865. (Author's collection)

From there it would continue its march through the night, passing north of the Union left flank, and heading west for 23 miles (37km) until it reached Farmville on the Southside Railroad in Prince Edward County. There Lee hoped to obtain supplies for his army, following which he would march south to Keysville along the Danville railroad.

As they struggled through the night, the weary Confederates had first to cross Flat Creek to reach Amelia Sulphur Springs, a once popular health resort. Finding the bridge across the creek collapsed, valuable time was lost as engineers repaired it to allow for the crossing of artillery and wagons.

A mounted column of the 1st New Jersey Cavalry approaches captured Confederate gun teams while dismounted troopers advance from the left in this engraving of the action near Paineville on April 5. Wounded Confederate infantry surrender in the foreground and the wagon train from Richmond can be seen in the distance. (*Battles & Leaders*)

Meanwhile, as the water was reasonably low, most of the infantry waded over to the opposite bank. Arriving at the springs, Lee learned from Commissary-General Isaac M. St. John that 80,000 rations originally sent to Burkeville, but returned once the Federal army advanced on that place, were now waiting at Farmville. Hence, St. John was instructed to proceed to Farmville and prepare for the issuance of the much-needed rations. Also during the course of that night, Lee gathered positive intelligence via dispatches seized from a captured Federal spy that Grant had indeed concentrated three army corps at Jetersville, and that Ord was in and around Burkeville; this confirmed that he was right to follow an alternative route west.

The head of the Confederate column reached Deatonsville and trudged on through the night across Sandy Creek and towards Little and Big Sailor's creeks, and Rice's Station on the Southside Railroad, after which it would turn north and cross the High Bridge over the Appomattox River. If Lee could cross and destroy this bridge, he might succeed in reaching Lynchburg and much-needed supplies.

As dawn broke on April 6, scouts on the left flank of Humphreys's II Corps observed the rearguard of Lee's column moving westward along a ridge on the opposite side of Flat Creek and orders were immediately issued to change direction. As the skirmishers of the 3rd Division, II Corps, waded across the river in pursuit, their commander, Brigadier-General Gershom Mott, was shot in the leg by a Confederate sharpshooter and carried to the rear, to be replaced by Brigadier-General Philip Régis de Trobriand. In the meantime, Sheridan's cavalry rode in three columns south of Jetersville and took the Pride's Church Road towards Deatonsville in order to pursue their prey. When beyond that place, elements of Crook's 2nd Division began a series of hit-and-run attacks on the Confederate wagon train and rearguard as the divisions of Custer and Devin arrived in support, with VI Corps marching not far behind. The V Corps was ordered to the right of the Union army, and in so doing was taken out of the fighting that day as it moved via Paineville and Rodophil, eventually encamping for the night near Ligontown Ferry having marched 32 miles (51km).

At the time of its construction in 1854, the chief engineer of the High Bridge across the Appomattox River, near Farmville, Virginia, remarked: "There have been higher bridges not so long, and longer bridges not so high, but taking the height and length together, this is, perhaps, the largest bridge in the world." Timothy H. O'Sullivan photographed the bridge while repairs were being conducted following its burning on April 6–7. (Library of Congress LC-DIG-ppmsca-33390)

As it became apparent to the Union high command that Lee was aiming for Lynchburg, Ord was instructed to maintain the bulk of his force at Burkeville but destroy any bridges that the Confederates might attempt to use. A prime target was High Bridge, a truss bridge that carried the Southside Railroad track across the flood plain in the broad but shallow valley cut by the Appomattox River. Completed in 1854, it rested on 20 abutments, and was 160ft (49m) above the river valley at its highest point with a span of nearly half a mile (800m). A much smaller wooden wagon bridge crossed the river a few hundred yards to the east. Ord believed both bridges to be poorly defended and, at about 4 a.m., sent a force consisting of the 54th Pennsylvania, commanded by Lieutenant-Colonel A.P. Moulton, and 123rd Ohio, of the Independent Division, XXIV Corps, plus companies I, L and M of the 4th Massachusetts Cavalry, to reconnoiter the area and burn High Bridge if it was not too well guarded. The entire expedition was initially commanded by Lieutenant-Colonel Horace Kellogg, with Colonel Francis Washburn leading the cavalry. Soon after, between 9 and 10 a.m., Ord received a dispatch from Sheridan warning that Lee's army might be heading his way. Consequently, he sent his chief of staff, Brigadier-General Theodore Read, accompanied by an orderly, to warn Kellogg and take command of the bridge-burning expedition.

Meanwhile, the head of the Confederate column, accompanied by Lee and Longstreet, began to arrive at Rice's Station on the Southside Railroad and, without realizing it, effectively cut off Read's command, which had already passed through on its way north to the High Bridge. When scouts reported the presence and apparent purpose of Read's expedition, Longstreet formed a defensive line along the ridge crossing the Rice Road near Pisgah Baptist Church, believing that a larger Union force might also stand between him and the bridge. He also ordered up all available cavalry. Arriving first with his division, Rosser was followed closely by that of Munford (Lee's Division), and the Confederate horsemen were tasked with stopping "the bridge-burners" if it took the last man to do it.

Although becoming aware of his predicament, Read continued on towards his goal. About a mile (1.6km) from the High Bridge, he halted the infantry in a narrow belt of woodland on the Chatham Plantation while Washburn's cavalry went forward to reconnoiter the area. Finding it much better defended than anticipated, Washburn saw two strong earthen redoubts either side of the road at each end of the bridge, with a lunette-style earthwork across the road about 100 yards (90m) in front of it. Still believing that a sudden attack on the rear of these defense works might carry the bridge, he sent his

troopers forward and they soon reached a smaller wooden bridge spanning the Sandy River, the planks of which had been torn up. Leading the advanced guard, 2nd Lieutenant George F. Davis dashed across the stream and relaid the planks under fire from the 3rd Virginia Reserves occupying the earthworks on the farther side. Washburn quickly came up with the main body and, crossing the bridge, threw out a line of skirmishers. He attacked so vigorously that, after a firefight lasting about a half hour, the Confederates retreated toward Farmville. There they were reinforced and Washburn soon found his troopers outnumbered and coming under heavy artillery fire. Moreover there was incessant musketry fire from the rear, which indicated that the infantry were also under attack, so he withdrew and went to their support.

The tracks of the Southside Railroad stretch about 2,400ft across the High Bridge. In this O'Sullivan photograph, the photographer poses at left while his assistant operates the camera. (Library of Congress LC-DIG-cwpb-01299)

Avoiding much of the road, Washburn led his men through the woods and along the bed of a ravine until he reached a hilltop overlooking the ensuing struggle. Realizing that the Pennsylvanian and Ohioan infantry, posted behind a fence along the edge of some woodland, were running out of ammunition and in danger of being overrun by a frontal attack from Munford's dismounted cavalry and a flank attack from the mounted brigades of Dearing and McCausland (Rosser's Division), he acted quickly. Leading his 79 officers and men around the right flank of the beleaguered Union infantry, he "wheeled to the left by fours" and charged headlong into Munford's dismounted troopers. Repulsed during the first attempt, the small battalion charged twice more, by which time Rosser's mounted brigades closed in on it and the action turned into a bloody, saber-wielding mêlée.

Of the first two clashes, Private George J. Hundley, 5th Virginia Cavalry (consolidated), recalled: "The enemy's cavalry charged that part of the line where I stood three times. They were mounted, and we dismounted. A single, well-directed volley scattered them each time, but the second time three Federal officers [probably Colonel Washburn and captains William T. Hodges (Company I) and John D.B. Goddard (Company L)] stood their ground, and attempted to cut their way out. We were not much more than a skirmish line, and here these three desperate men came down right amongst us, whilst our men were reloading, cutting and slashing with their sabres as they came. A sight so unusual puzzled our men at first, but soon finding these fellows to be in earnest, some one cried out, 'Kill the d----d Yankees,' and instantly the three men went down as if they had suddenly melted away. I remember seeing the dust fly from their coats behind as the bullets passed through their bodies."

Of the Union losses, Washburn fell from his horse with a gunshot wound to the mouth, following which he received a saber cut across the skull. Found with the dead and wounded by the Army of the James the following day, he died of his wounds 16 days later. Captains Hodges and Goddard both appear to have been killed instantly. Of the enlisted men, only two were killed while four of the 60 captured were wounded. Reports on Confederate casualties do not survive, although Major Edward T. Bouvé, 4th Massachusetts Cavalry, commented that their loss was "at least a half greater in number than Washburn's whole force."

Fierce fighting also occurred as the Union infantry were forced back by sheer weight of numbers to the High Bridge, where many of them threw down their weapons and surrendered. Refusing to do so, Brigadier-General James Read was shot dead by Brigadier-General Dearing, who also fell mortally wounded at the same time. Four men were killed and one wounded in the 54th Pennsylvania, while the 123rd Ohio sustained only one man killed. A total of 780 Union prisoners were taken. All but one remained

A "glass blower" before the war, Private Richard Cunningham (Company I, 4th Massachusetts Cavalry) took part in the failed bridge burning expedition and crucial cavalry battle of High Bridge during the attempt to cut off the retreat of the Army of Northern Virginia on April 6. According to his own account, he was "the only man [of his command] who escaped capture on the occasion of the High Bridge affair." (Courtesy of descendent Matthew Wallace-Gross)

in captivity for just three days and were released upon the surrender of the Army of Northern Virginia.

The action at High Bridge was considered by many to have been a useless sacrifice. Although they failed in their objective of destroying the bridge and preventing the escape of Lee's army across the Appomattox River, the bravery and determination of the "bridge-burning" expedition did hasten the termination of the war in Virginia. After the surrender, Lee's Inspector General, Samuel Cooper, commented: "To the sharpness of that fight, the cutting off of Lee's army at Appomattox Court House was probably owing. So fierce were the charges of Colonel Washburn and his men, and so determined their fighting, that General Lee received the impression that they must be supported by a large portion of the army, and that his retreat was cut off." As a result, the Army of Northern Virginia had halted and begun to entrench at Rice's Station. This delay allowed Ord's Army of the James to close up with Lee, which denied him the option of a direct southerly escape route and forced him to detour further west by way of Appomattox Court House. It also enabled Sheridan to intercept the Confederates at Little Sailor's Creek.

Little Sailor's Creek, April 6

As the Confederates continued to arrive at Rice's Station during the morning of April 6, Anderson's Corps was discovered by Crook's scouts at about 11 a.m. moving along the Rice–Deatonsville Road and the 3rd Brigade, commanded by Colonel Charles H. Smith, of Crook's 2nd Division was ordered to attack it. As a result, Anderson halted to protect the main wagon trains following behind; this created a critical gap in the Confederate column between him and Longstreet. This in turn caused Anderson to order Pickett's Division to throw up temporary breastworks, behind which they kept Crook's troopers at bay and forced them to withdraw.

By about 2 p.m., after crossing over Little Sailor's Creek at Gill's Mill, Custer also became aware of the gap between Anderson and Longstreet near Marshall's Crossroads. Observing Huger's artillery battalion attempting to pass through the break in the line, he swept down on it, capturing most of the guns. With the arrival of elements of Pickett's infantry, Custer next withdrew to await infantry reinforcements which were approaching in the form of VI Corps. Wright's troops had passed south of Deatonsville along the Pride's Church Road, following which they headed west across open country towards the road along which the Confederate column was moving. Seeing the Union battle lines approaching, the Confederate infantry attempted to throw up breastworks but retreated west along the road, while the remaining wagons were forced to turn north along a lane leading to the Jamestown Road with Gordon's Division acting as rearguard. In so doing they moved into the path of II Corps, which was also rapidly moving west from Deatonsville. Meanwhile, Anderson crossed Little Sailor's Creek near the Hillsman Farm only to find further elements of Crook's cavalry blocking his way to Rice's Station.

Commanding elements of the 4th Massachusetts Cavalry, Colonel Francis Washburn died following the charge he led at High Bridge on April 6. (*The Fourth Massachusetts Cavalry*)

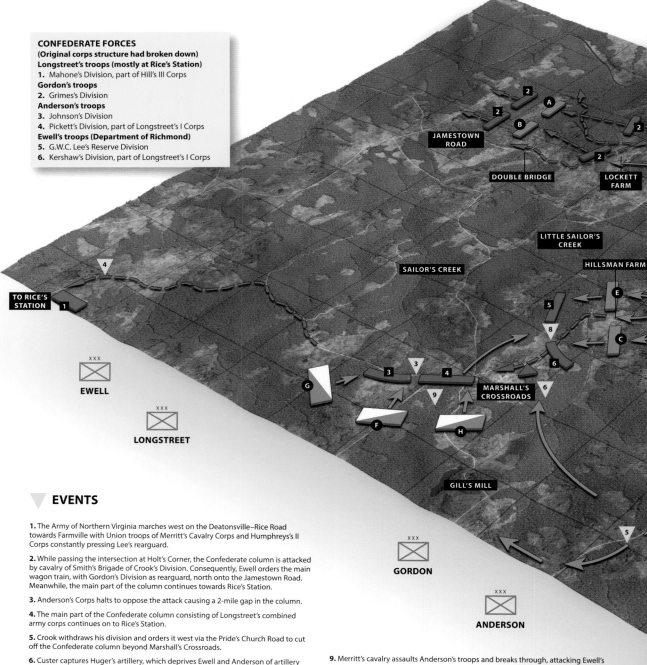

CONFEDERATE FORCES
(Original corps structure had broken down)
Longstreet's troops (mostly at Rice's Station)
1. Mahone's Division, part of Hill's III Corps
Gordon's troops
2. Grimes's Division
Anderson's troops
3. Johnson's Division
4. Pickett's Division, part of Longstreet's I Corps
Ewell's troops (Department of Richmond)
5. G.W.C. Lee's Reserve Division
6. Kershaw's Division, part of Longstreet's I Corps

JAMESTOWN ROAD

DOUBLE BRIDGE

LOCKETT FARM

LITTLE SAILOR'S CREEK

SAILOR'S CREEK

HILLSMAN FARM

TO RICE'S STATION

XXX
EWELL

XXX
LONGSTREET

MARSHALL'S CROSSROADS

GILL'S MILL

XXX
GORDON

XXX
ANDERSON

EVENTS

1. The Army of Northern Virginia marches west on the Deatonsville–Rice Road towards Farmville with Union troops of Merritt's Cavalry Corps and Humphreys's II Corps constantly pressing Lee's rearguard.

2. While passing the intersection at Holt's Corner, the Confederate column is attacked by cavalry of Smith's Brigade of Crook's Division. Consequently, Ewell orders the main wagon train, with Gordon's Division as rearguard, north onto the Jamestown Road. Meanwhile, the main part of the column continues towards Rice's Station.

3. Anderson's Corps halts to oppose the attack causing a 2-mile gap in the column.

4. The main part of the Confederate column consisting of Longstreet's combined army corps continues on to Rice's Station.

5. Crook withdraws his division and orders it west via the Pride's Church Road to cut off the Confederate column beyond Marshall's Crossroads.

6. Custer captures Huger's artillery, which deprives Ewell and Anderson of artillery support.

7. Wright's VI Corps marches along the Pride's Church Road and turns west across open country to attack the Confederate column on the Deatonsville–Rice Road.

8. Ewell's troops make a stand near the Hillsman Farmhouse and west of Little Sailor's Creek, but without artillery are overwhelmed and captured by Wright's Corps.

9. Merritt's cavalry assaults Anderson's troops and breaks through, attacking Ewell's rear.

10. Humphreys's II Corps pursues and catches up with the main Confederate wagon train near the double bridge and Lockett's Farm. "Rooney" Lee's cavalry is ordered forward to protect the High Bridge, which exposes Gordon's rearguard. Humphreys's troops attack and force Gordon's infantry west of Little Sailor's Creek, capturing the wagon train and forcing the Confederates to either surrender or run.

BATTLES OF LITTLE SAILOR'S CREEK, APRIL 6, 1865

After the fall of Petersburg and Richmond, Lee's army attempts to escape to North Carolina to join forces with Joseph E. Johnston's army, but the rear of his column, including his main wagon train, is attacked and destroyed at four separate locations in collectively what has become known as the Battles of Little Sailor's Creek.

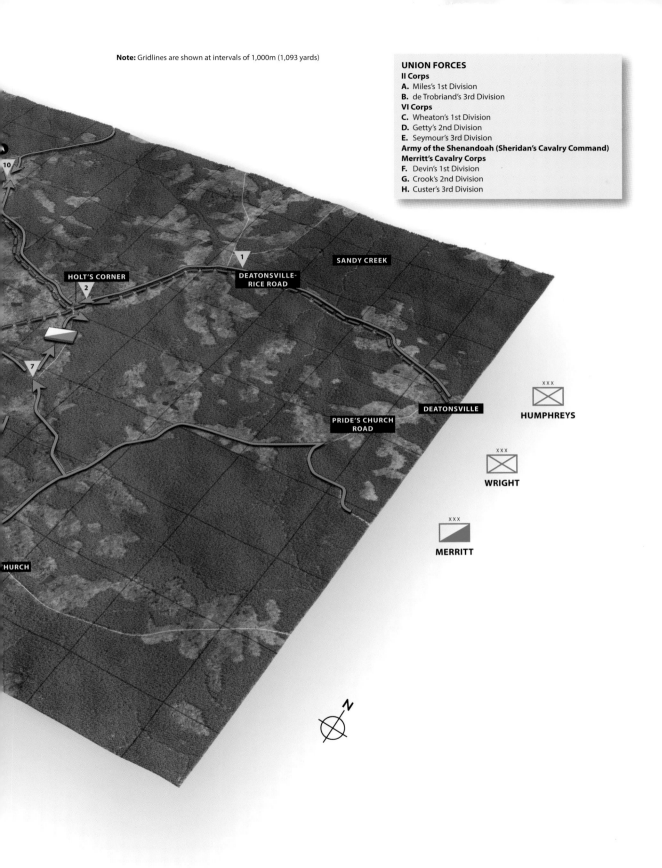

Note: Gridlines are shown at intervals of 1,000m (1,093 yards)

UNION FORCES
II Corps
A. Miles's 1st Division
B. de Trobriand's 3rd Division
VI Corps
C. Wheaton's 1st Division
D. Getty's 2nd Division
E. Seymour's 3rd Division
Army of the Shenandoah (Sheridan's Cavalry Command)
Merritt's Cavalry Corps
F. Devin's 1st Division
G. Crook's 2nd Division
H. Custer's 3rd Division

10

HOLT'S CORNER

2

1

DEATONSVILLE-
RICE ROAD

SANDY CREEK

7

PRIDE'S CHURCH
ROAD

DEATONSVILLE

HURCH

xxx
HUMPHREYS

xxx
WRIGHT

xxx
MERRITT

N

As the wagons departed the main Confederate column, Ewell realized he would have to make a stand. Posting Fitzgerald's Mississippi Brigade and the dismounted 24th Virginia Cavalry as his rearguard, he moved his Reserve Corps amounting to only about 4,000 men to the hillside on the opposite bank of Little Sailor's Creek, which one Union soldier described as "a stream of muddy water a dozen feet wide." There he formed them into a semicircular line of battle, the convexity of which faced northeast towards the approaching enemy with G.W.C. Lee's small division on the left and Kershaw's Division on the right. Tucker's Naval Brigade held the position behind Lee's men. Edged with scrub pine, the creek was about 300 yards (300m) to his front, and the ground on the opposite bank was clear for about 800 yards (730m) towards the Hillsman Farmhouse, which would serve as a field hospital during and after the ensuing battle.

Ewell rode over to confer with the now halted Anderson regarding the impending action. Either they could unite their forces and attempt to breach the cavalry roadblock, or strike off through woodland and open country until they reached the road to Farmville. Before they could come to a decision, Wright's VI Corps appeared at Ewell's front having advanced west along the road, commencing what became known as the Battles of Little Sailor's Creek. Sheridan took command of the Union VI Corps infantry at this stage and placed Wheaton's 1st Division on the left of the line of battle with Seymour's 3rd Division on the right, and Getty's 2nd Division in reserve. According to Major Franklin Harwood, commanding the Battalion of Engineers attached to VI Corps, the Confederate position was "densely timbered, except one open space of about 100 yards width, across which their line was plainly visible, lying down."

Meanwhile, Merritt prepared his three cavalry divisions to attack Anderson's troops, who were digging in behind breastworks along the road to Rice's Station, with Pickett's Division on the left and that of Bushrod Johnson on the right. Thus, the forces of Ewell and Anderson formed a right angle with Union infantry to their northeast and Union cavalry to the south. As Huger's artillery had been captured and all other ordnance was with the wagon train, the Confederates could make no response to the Federal artillery shells which began to rain in on them at about 5.15 p.m. Major Harwood commented: "From our commanding position three or four batteries were brought to bear on this exposed position of their line, which was cut up terribly by our plunging fire of shell and case-shot." Following a half-hour bombardment, Wheaton's infantry advanced in line of battle towards Little Sailor's Creek, pushing back Ewell's skirmishers. Many of them taunted the Confederates by waving handkerchiefs, trying to induce them to surrender.

The Union infantrymen crossed the creek at two places with difficulty due to its depth caused by heavy spring rainfall and its swampy condition. As they reformed on the opposite bank and continued their advance, Ewell's troops

Based on a painting by Gilbert Gaul, this engraving depicts a Confederate officer urging embattled infantrymen to save their battle flag following the collapse of Kershaw's Division near Hillsman Farmhouse at Little Sailor's Creek on April 6. (*Battles & Leaders*)

rose from behind their breastworks and fired a volley. Commanding the 3rd Division, VI Corps, Brigadier-General Truman Seymour reported: "the Confederate Marine Battalion fought with peculiar obstinacy, and our lines, somewhat disordered by crossing the creek, were repulsed in the first onset." Following this, some of G.W.C. Lee's men got caught up in the excitement of the moment and launched a counterattack, which panicked the Pennsylvanians and Rhode Islanders of Edward's 3rd Brigade (Wheaton's 1st Division). Hand-to-hand fighting ensued as some of the Union troops were chased back into the creek, sustaining 373 killed and wounded. According to Confederate Major Robert Stiles, who was captured that day: "The battle degenerated into a butchery of brutal personal conflicts. I saw ... men kill each other with bayonets and the butts of muskets, and even bite each other's throats and ears and noses, rolling on the ground like wild beasts." Although Confederate losses are not known, Colonel Stapleton Crutchfield (of G.W.C. Lee's Division) was shot in the head and died instantly during the frenzied action. Eventually, Union artillery opened up with canister and forced the Confederates back behind their breastworks.

Attacking concurrently with Wright's VI Corps, Merritt's cavalry advanced on Anderson's line south of the Rice's Station road, with Crook hitting the Confederate right flank,while the remaining two divisions stormed the Confederate front. As Gregg's dismounted brigade of Crook's 2nd Division forced Bushrod Johnson's troops back, Custer led several charges against Pickett's men and finally broke through, shattering the lines of the Confederate infantry which ran towards the woods or west towards Lee's main column at Rice's Station. Custer's cavalry then began to veer right into the rear of Ewell's troops as the infantry of Wright's corps launched a second attack. This flanked Kershaw's troops on the Confederate right and, with the support of the cavalry, overran much of Ewell's line due to sheer weight of numbers.

Known as the "Black Thursday of the Confederacy," out of a total of 3,600 men under Ewell's command 150 were killed or wounded, and 3,250 were captured or missing. Furthermore, six generals, consisting of Ewell, G.W.C. Lee, Joseph Kershaw, Seth Barton, Dudley DuBose and James Sims, were captured. Of the 6,300 men with Anderson, a total of 2,600 were killed, wounded or captured. Included in the latter were generals Eppa Hunton and Montgomery Corse.

Meanwhile, de Trobriand's 3rd Division led II Corps in pursuit of the main Confederate wagon train still rumbling along the Jamestown Road, forcing Gordon's rearguard to make a stand at every possible opportunity. At Deatonsville Gordon's troops, supported by "Rooney" Lee's cavalry, threw up breastworks and fended off an attack at a cost of about 400 men captured plus one battle flag lost. The running fight continued until they reached the bridges near the confluence of Little and Big Sailor's creeks at about 5 p.m., by which time Lee's cavalry had been ordered west to protect the High Bridge, leaving Gordon's infantry exposed to further attack. Furthermore, the wagons became congested and bogged down in the mud, and the infantry was forced to rapidly form yet another defensive line on the Lockett Farm about a half mile from the river crossings as Humphreys's troops closed in around them. Attacked simultaneously by the divisions of de Trobriand and Miles, Gordon's men finally abandoned most of the wagons and fell back to the high ground across the creek where many of them began to surrender, while others pushed on towards Farmville as darkness descended.

THE NAVAL BRIGADE AT LITTLE SAILOR'S CREEK, APRIL 6, 1865 (PP. 70–71)

Tucker's Naval Brigade **(1)** was the last of Ewell's troops to lay down their arms at Little Sailor's Creek. Of their part in the battle, Union Major-General Horatio Wright commented in his report: "I was never more astonished. These troops were surrounded … my artillery and a fresh division in their front **(2)**, and some three divisions of Major-General Sheridan's cavalry in their rear **(3)**. Looking upon them as already our prisoners, I had ordered the artillery to cease firing as a dictate of humanity; my surprise therefore was extreme when this force charged upon our front." A humble Confederate soldier recalled: "I was next to those Marines and saw them fight. They clubbed muskets, fired pistols into each other's face and used bayonets savagely." Major Robert Stiles, of the Confederate artillery, remembered seeing one of his comrades and "a Federal officer fighting with swords over the battalion colors … each having his left hand on the staff," but the

Southerner was a "very athletic, powerful seaman," and soon he "saw the Federal officer fall" **(4)**. A member of Phillips' Georgia Legion recalled: "those marines fought like tigers and against odds of at least ten to one."

Reluctant to accept they were beaten, Tucker's brigade fell back "into the dense timber in a depression in the bluffs" and eventually surrendered after several attempts by Union officers to persuade them to do so. According to Captain McHenry Howard, Assistant Inspector General of G.W.C. Lee's division, the Federals were "greatly astonished at the miscellaneous uniforms" worn by the artillerists, seamen and marines in Custis Lee's command, and when the naval uniform was pointed out, exclaimed "Good heaven! Have you gunboats way up here, too?"

The day concluded with approximately 1,700 prisoners taken by II Corps, plus 13 battle flags, 3 pieces of artillery, and over 300 wagons and 70 field ambulances. Humphreys's II Corps camped on the battlefield, while the farmhouse owned by James S. Lockett was commandeered as a field hospital for the wounded. As a result of the three actions collectively known as the Battles of Little Sailor's Creek, which were the last major battles of the war in Virginia, Lee lost the leadership of eight generals while approximately 7,700 Confederate soldiers, sailors and marines had surrendered or were captured; by this time, this amounted to almost one-fifth of what remained of the Army of Northern Virginia. Union losses in VI Corps were about 440 officers and men.

As the cannon and musket fire subsided, Lee anxiously enquired about the status of the rear of his column and wagon train, and rode back towards the battlefield with the remains of Mahone's Division to ascertain the situation. Seeing survivors streaming along the road, he exclaimed, "My God, has the army dissolved?" to which Mahone replied, "No, General, here are troops ready to do their duty." The General-in-Chief replied, "Yes, there are still some true men left … Will you please keep those people back?"

On the Union side, Sheridan sent a message to Grant, who had reached Burkeville, stating: "If the thing is pressed, I think that Lee will surrender." When Sheridan's report reached Lincoln at City Point, he responded: "Let the thing be pressed."

Before continuing on to Rice's Station, Lee placed Mahone in charge of the remains of Anderson's troops with instructions to lead them across the Appomattox River at High Bridge under cover of darkness. Gordon was also advised by a courier to follow suit if he could escape. Once on the north side of the river, these men were to burn both the railroad and wagon bridges to prevent the enemy from following them. As it was generally not possible to ford the Appomattox in that area, the Federal pursuit would be delayed while they awaited the arrival of a pontoon bridge. Upon return to his headquarters at Rice's Station, Lee received a dispatch from Davis at Danville, asking if there was an objective point for the army. Lee replied: "No; I shall have to be governed by each day's developments … A few more Sailor's Creeks and it will all be over."

In order to outdistance the Union forces once again and feed his army with the subsistence waiting at Farmville, Lee ordered Longstreet to commence another night march with Field's Division leading the way, followed by Heth and Wilcox, with the cavalry guarding the rear. If they could reach Farmville unmolested and distribute the rations, his men could then cross to the north side of the Appomattox via the railroad bridge above the town as Mahone and Gordon were passing over High Bridge 4 miles (6.4km) northeast. Lee could then have both bridges destroyed, which would further hamper the Union pursuit as he moved on to Appomattox Station where additional rations awaited.

Custer prepares for his third charge against Pickett's Division at Marshall's Crossroads during the Battles of Little Sailor's Creek on April 6. The notation on the verso of this drawing by Alfred Waud reads: "Custer charged and charged again here capturing and destroying trains and making many prisoners. On the left are his guns engaging the enemy." (Library of Congress LC-USZ62-14654)

Reaching Farmville during the early hours of April 7, the Confederates found the supply trains sent earlier from Burkeville awaiting them. As a result, about 40,000 rations of bread and 80,000 of meal were issued. The famished troops also gorged themselves on delicacies such as whole hams and French soup packaged in tin foil. The problem for Lee was ensuring as much food as possible was distributed before the Union army closed in on them again. After a brief conference with Secretary of War Breckinridge, Quartermaster-General Alexander R. Lawton, and Commissary-General St. John, Lee got some much-needed rest at the home of wealthy tobacconist Patrick Jackson on Beech Street in Farmville.

Cumberland Church, April 7

After bivouacking overnight on the battlefields at Little Sailor's Creek, the Federals continued their pursuit the next morning. Humphreys's II Corps and Wright's VI Corps were put in motion at 5.30 a.m. Coming along behind them was Griffin's V Corps which had started its march from near Ligontown at 5 a.m. Sheridan moved around to the south of Farmville with the divisions of Custer and Devin, while Crook's cavalry was in advance of the infantry.

Meanwhile, the Confederates had problems destroying High Bridge and the smaller wagon bridge nearby. Riding ahead of Mahone's troops during the night, Anderson placed sentinels at each end of both bridges with orders to let no one else pass and that stragglers should be gathered south of the river. Hence, time was wasted while Mahone found Anderson and gained clearance for his troops and wagons to cross. As his exhausted men halted for rest on the opposite bank, Mahone again found Anderson and Gordon and, as it seemed the end might be near, suggested the possibility of surrendering their troops. As a result, Anderson was delegated to convey these sentiments to Longstreet, but there is no evidence that this happened. At the same time, Gordon agreed to order the Engineers under Colonel Thomas M. Talcott to burn the bridges, but this was not attempted until after daylight on April 7, shortly after which the skirmishers of the 19th Maine Infantry, the lead unit of Barlow's 2nd Division (II Corps), began arriving at the scene. After the last Confederate troops had crossed High Bridge, the garrison blew up one of the redoubts guarding its southeastern approaches. Meanwhile, the Maine men ran on to the lower wagon bridge just as the flames were beginning to take hold at the far end. While some put up a screen of defensive fire, others dowsed the flames, which permitted the rest of Olmsted's 1st Brigade to cross. At the same time, the pioneers of Barlow's division attempted to extinguish the fire on High Bridge, which had already taken hold on the first four spans and was beginning to weaken the fifth, which finally collapsed; their action prevented the fire from

This pencil sketch on tan paper by Alfred Waud depicts Ewell's Corps of Local Defense troops surrendering near the Hillsman Farm during the Battles of Sailor's Creek on April 6. The artist wrote on the reverse: "This was quite an effective incident in its way. The soldiers silhoutted [sic] against the western sky with their muskets thrown butt upwards in token of surrender, as our troops closed in beyond a wagon train which was captured." The wagons shown were probably the tail end of Mahone's Division. (Library of Congress LC-USZ62-14654)

the last of Ewells Corps april 6

Description on back.

74

The Battle of Cumberland Church, April 7, 1865.

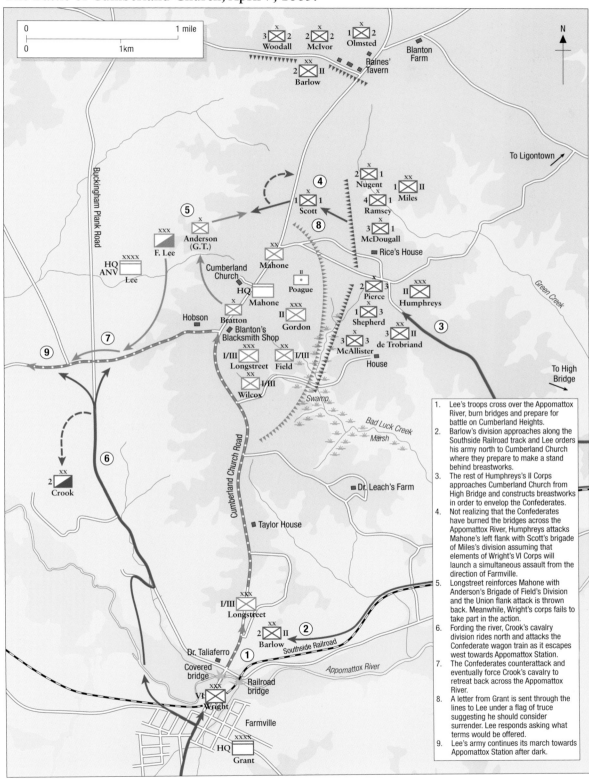

1. Lee's troops cross over the Appomattox River, burn bridges and prepare for battle on Cumberland Heights.
2. Barlow's division approaches along the Southside Railroad track and Lee orders his army north to Cumberland Church where they prepare to make a stand behind breastworks.
3. The rest of Humphreys's II Corps approaches Cumberland Church from High Bridge and constructs breastworks in order to envelop the Confederates.
4. Not realizing that the Confederates have burned the bridges across the Appomattox River, Humphreys attacks Mahone's left flank with Scott's brigade of Miles's division assuming that elements of Wright's VI Corps will launch a simultaneous assault from the direction of Farmville.
5. Longstreet reinforces Mahone with Anderson's Brigade of Field's Division and the Union flank attack is thrown back. Meanwhile, Wright's corps fails to take part in the action.
6. Fording the river, Crook's cavalry division rides north and attacks the Confederate wagon train as it escapes west towards Appomattox Station.
7. The Confederates counterattack and eventually force Crook's cavalry to retreat back across the Appomattox River.
8. A letter from Grant is sent through the lines to Lee under a flag of truce suggesting he should consider surrender. Lee responds asking what terms would be offered.
9. Lee's army continues its march towards Appomattox Station after dark.

devouring the rest of the structure. Mahone's troops then tried to retake the wagon bridge, but were thrown back with the arrival of Miles's division.

Crossing the charred wagon bridge, Miles's and de Trobriand's men next pursued Mahone's column, which withdrew along the Jamestown Road, while Barlow headed after Gordon's column as it marched along the railroad track to Farmville. Approaching too close to the Confederate rearguard, Brigadier-General Thomas A. Smyth, commanding the 3rd Brigade, 2nd Division, II Corps, was shot dead by enemy fire during this part of the pursuit. Barlow ordered his troops to halt once they reached the outskirts of Farmville, having passed 135 burning wagons destroyed by the Confederates.

Near the railroad station on the northern edge of town, Longstreet's chief of artillery Brigadier-General Edward P. Alexander ordered the wagon and railroad bridges to be burned before the Union troops could reach them. Although successful, this act was premature, as not all the Confederate troops had crossed over, and Rosser's and Munford's cavalry, plus the infantrymen of Bratton's Brigade of Field's Division, were forced to ford the river further upstream. Those who got over the Appomattox moved to high ground known as Cumberland Heights, with the artillery shelling Wright's VI Corps as it approached Farmville. Meanwhile, the infantry faced east in preparation to fight Barlow's approaching troops, only to be ordered several miles further north to Cumberland Presbyterian Church. Crook's cavalry entered Farmville at about 1.30 p.m. and moved towards the river, which they forded slightly west of the town limits, before riding west along the Buckingham Plank Road. Ord's Army of the James arrived in the town next, followed by Wright's corps.

At this late stage Alexander advised Lee that, in order to reach their next destination at Appomattox Station, it would have been a much shorter march of 30 miles (50km) if the army had remained south of the river and progressed along the road running parallel with the Southside Railroad. As it was, they now faced a march of 38 miles (61km) via New Store and Appomattox Court House while Grant's forces had less distance to travel via Walker's Church or Pamplin Station, and could cut him off. To make matters worse, Lee also learned that the enemy had crossed at High Bridge, and were on the same side of the river as he was. Thus, any hope of breaking contact with them was now at an end.

As Mahone's 3,500 troops reached the high ground around Cumberland Church, they were ordered to cover the progress of the wagon train by entrenching and throwing up a line of breastworks with Poague's artillery battalion on their right. As the remainder of Lee's army appeared, Gordon's corps followed by Longstreet's corps occupied Mahone's right, forming a giant fish-hook shape facing north and east with the church in the center behind them. The exhausted Confederates dug in along a slight ridge with a series of rolling hills and valleys at their front. As the lead elements of Miles's 1st Division arrived at about 2 p.m., Scott's 1st Brigade was ordered to attempt to turn Mahone's left flank while Wright's VI Corps was to attack the Confederate rear from the south having advanced from Farmville. However, Humphreys was unaware that the bridges had been destroyed and that the VI Corps infantry was unable to cross the river. Scott's troops advanced with fixed bayonets at about 4.15 p.m. and the Confederates poured musket and cannon fire into their ranks. Some of the Union soldiers managed to reach the enemy breastworks, only to be captured; others began to turn Mahone's flank and got in his rear, only to be repulsed by the Georgia Brigade of Brigadier-General George Anderson (Field's Division), who were ordered forward as reinforcements by Longstreet. According to Mahone's very brief after-battle report, two assaults were "handsomely repulsed" with little Confederate loss while "the enemy were most severely punished."

Meanwhile farther south, after fording the Appomattox, Crook's cavalry division discovered the Confederate wagon train about a half mile southwest of Cumberland Church heading towards Appomattox Station. Leading Crook's column, the 4th Pennsylvania Cavalry of Gregg's 2nd Brigade was ordered to attack, but as they rode into the line of lumbering wagons, elements of Munford's cavalry struck them on their right flank, dismounting and capturing General J. Irvin Gregg and causing the Union troopers to panic and run. According to Private Carlton McCarthy, 2nd Company of Richmond Howitzers, Gregg was "splendidly equipped and greatly admired by the ragged crowd around him." Colonel Samuel Young managed to rally the scattered remains of Gregg's command and with support from Davies's 1st Brigade and Battery A, 2nd US Artillery, renewed the attack on the wagons. On this occasion they were met by Lewis's North Carolinian infantry brigade backed by the guns of Owens's artillery battalion. In the bloody encounter which ensued, Confederate Brigadier-General William Lewis was severely wounded and captured, and Robert E. Lee, who witnessed the action which took place close to his headquarters, attempted to lead a charge himself. Seeing their beloved commanding general coming under fire, the Confederate troops nearby are believed to have cried out: "No, no, but if you will retire we will do the work." Following further intense resistance, Crook's cavalry troopers retreated and were driven back across the river.

At his headquarters in Farmville, Grant decided to begin communications with Lee about the possibility of surrender. At 5 p.m. on April 7, he wrote: "The results of the last week must convince you of the hopelessness of further resistance on the part of the Army of Northern Virginia in this struggle. I feel that it is so, and regard it as my duty to shift from myself the responsibility of any further effusion of bloodshed, by asking of you the surrender of that portion of the C.S. Army known as the Army of Northern Virginia." This message was carried by Brigadier-General Seth Williams, of Grant's staff, via High Bridge and passed under a flag of truce to Captain Herman Perry, adjutant general of Sorrel's Brigade, Mahone's Division. It was handed to Lee at about 9.30 p.m. After silently studying the document, Lee passed it to Longstreet, after which he replied: "Not yet." Composing his response, he wrote that he disagreed with Grant's view that the Confederate situation was hopeless, but reciprocated his "desire to avoid useless effusion of blood," and asked the Union commander what terms would be offered if he agreed to surrender his army.

Realizing he must make another night march if he was to continue his withdrawal, he next issued orders for his troops to silently leave their earthworks at 11 p.m. Lee's plan was to reach Appomattox Station, issue rations and supplies, and then march west to Campbell Court House, from where he would hopefully at last be able to head south to Danville. Once at the latter point, the remains of his army might still manage to link up with Johnston's forces in North Carolina. As his troops were now reduced to only Longstreet's combined corps and Gordon's corps, the two left Cumberland Church via separate routes. Longstreet's corps marched north for about 5 miles (8km) along the Buckingham Plank Road and then turned west towards Curdsville. Gordon's corps took a parallel route along the Lynchburg Wagon Road, eventually heading for New Store with Fitzhugh Lee's cavalry as a rearguard.

Appomattox Station, April 8

The next day passed relatively quietly for both armies. Finding that Lee had abandoned his works around Cumberland Church, the Union II and VI corps continued their pursuit, the latter finally having crossed the Appomattox River via a pontoon bridge. Wright's corps followed after Longstreet while Humphreys's fell in behind Gordon. What was left of Anderson's Corps was combined with those of Gordon's. As Gordon's route was slightly shorter, his column reached New Store before that of Longstreet, and consequently II/IV Corps was in the van with I/II Corps bringing up the rear after joining forces at New Store Presbyterian Church. During the afternoon of this march, Lee relieved generals Richard Anderson, George Pickett and Bushrod Johnson from duty, probably because their commands were so few in numbers since Little Sailor's Creek. It appears that the latter two were never informed of their dismissal, or chose to ignore it as they were still with the army at Appomattox the next day. Anderson did leave with orders to proceed home and was to report to Secretary of War Breckinridge.

By this time exhaustion combined with lack of food and proper sleep was taking its toll on what remained of the rank and file of the Army of Northern Virginia. While some men continued to trudge on behind their officers, others quietly slipped away when they came to a road that might lead eventually to their homes and families. At about 9 a.m. a second message sent by Grant reached the rear of the Confederate column. Passed along the line, it was not finally handed to Lee until late in the afternoon. Regarding terms of surrender, it stated simply that the surrendering troops should not bear arms "against the Government of the United States until properly exchanged." He also offered to meet Lee to discuss the conditions for surrender.

Later, at about 4 p.m., the Union II Corps, having marched the shorter route, closed on the rear of Gordon's column, and arrived at New Store before VI Corps. Meanwhile south of the Appomattox River, the other wing of Grant's army progressed along the shorter route to Appomattox Station intending to cut off Lee's troops, just as Confederate General Alexander had predicted. Prior to leaving his headquarters at Buffalo Creek, Sheridan reported to Grant: "the enemy must have taken the fine road north of the Appomattox River. I will move on Appomattox Court House." Later that day Grant responded: "I think Lee will surrender to-day. I addressed him on the subject last evening, and received a reply this morning asking the terms I wanted. We will push him until terms are agreed upon." Sheridan's

Having served in the Otey Battery, 13th Battalion Virginia Light Artillery, since November 5, 1863, Private W.S. Pilcher chose not to participate in the surrender of the Army of Northern Virginia. He did not make it very far before deciding it would be best to turn himself over to Union authorities, and was paroled in Lynchburg, Virginia, only about 30 miles (50km) west of Appomattox Court House, on April 13, 1865. (Courtesy of the Appomattox Court House National Historical Park)

The Battle of Appomattox Station, April 8, 1865.

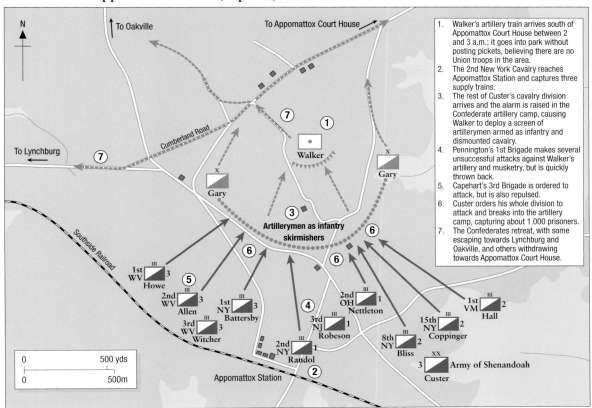

N
To Oakville
To Appomattox Court House

1. Walker's artillery train arrives south of Appomattox Court House between 2 and 3 a.m.; it goes into park without posting pickets, believing there are no Union troops in the area.
2. The 2nd New York Cavalry reaches Appomattox Station and captures three supply trains.
3. The rest of Custer's cavalry division arrives and the alarm is raised in the Confederate artillery camp, causing Walker to deploy a screen of artillerymen armed as infantry and dismounted cavalry.
4. Pennington's 1st Brigade makes several unsuccessful attacks against Walker's artillery and musketry, but is quickly thrown back.
5. Capehart's 3rd Brigade is ordered to attack, but is also repulsed.
6. Custer orders his whole division to attack and breaks into the artillery camp, capturing about 1,000 prisoners.
7. The Confederates retreat, with some escaping towards Lynchburg and Oakville, and others withdrawing towards Appomattox Court House.

Cumberland Road

To Lynchburg

Walker

Gary

Gary

Artillerymen as infantry skirmishers

Southside Railroad

1st WV 3 Howe
2nd WV 3 Allen
1st NY 3 Battersby
3rd WV 3 Witcher
2nd NY 1 Randol
3rd NJ 1 Robeson
2nd OH 1 Nettleton
8th NY 2 Bliss
15th NY 2 Coppinger
1st VM 2 Hall
3 Army of Shenandoah
Custer

0   500 yds
0   500m

Appomattox Station

scouts also informed him that supplies had been dispatched to Lee from Lynchburg to Appomattox Station along the Southside Railroad in four trains. All of his cavalry commanders were informed of this new information and ordered to press forward with haste. Crook followed the road alongside the Southside Railroad tracks and after an 8-mile (13km) ride from Farmville arrived at Prospect Station, following which one of his troopers remarked: "we found neither station nor prospect." Coming along behind, Sheridan

Pilcher wore this Richmond Depot Type III jacket during the Appomattox Campaign. Made from cadet gray wool kersey, it has a six-piece body and two-piece sleeves and was fastened by nine wooden buttons. (Courtesy of the Appomattox Court House National Historical Park)

with the Army of the Shenandoah cavalry turned off and headed northwest towards Walker's Church. Continuing on to Pamplin Station, Crook captured three engines and accompanying rolling stock, plus boxes of muskets. North of the river, the artillery wagon train commanded by Brigadier-General R.L. Walker headed for Appomattox Station with no idea that Federal cavalry was heading in the same direction.

Reaching Walker's Church, Sheridan sent a dispatch to Crook advising that the rest of the cavalry would join him at Appomattox Station, and that if he got there first he must destroy the enemy trains. Crossing Sawney's Creek, Sheridan continued on for another 12 miles (19km) with Merritt's column until he arrived in the vicinity of the station. Meanwhile, the infantry followed behind with the Army of the James moving from Farmville to Prospect Station and V Corps converging on the same depot via Hampden-Sydney College. Marching on either side of the road to permit the flow of artillery, wagons and ambulances, Ord's infantry fell in behind Merritt's cavalry while Griffin's troops brought up the rear. As they marched along, Ord urged them on at various points with rallying cries such as "Legs will win this battle, men."

At the head of Custer's column as it approached Appomattox Station was the 2nd New York Cavalry, which found three supply trains from Lynchburg as expected. A fourth managed to escape when its crew spied the approaching Union troopers. The three captured trains were taken by only a small detachment of Union cavalry who faced no resistance from the crews and nearby engineer troops. As the doors of the boxcars were slid open, the Union troopers found 300,000 rations, plus other supplies including uniforms, shoes, blankets and medical supplies. The captured trains were moved to the east.

About a mile farther north, Walker's artillery and wagon train had reached Appomattox Court House between 2 p.m. and 3 p.m., with Gordon's corps behind them. Halting 2 miles (3km) west of the Court House Walker failed to post pickets, believing there were no Union troops in the area, while his only support consisted of Gary's small cavalry brigade which was mostly dismounted. So close to the supply trains at Appomattox Station, the exhausted artillerymen looked forward to their first proper meal at daylight. Around 4 p.m. the alarm was raised in the artillery camp with cries of "Yankees! Sheridan!" and "The cavalry are coming, they are at the station and coming up the hill!" Walker hastily formed Gary's cavalrymen on either flank and placed his guns, amounting to about 30 pieces, on a low ridge in a convex semicircle facing towards the station. He also threw out a screen of skirmishers consisting of artillerymen armed as infantry. Meanwhile, his other 70 guns continued to escape in the direction of Auray. Consisting of densely overgrown

This photograph by Timothy O'Sullivan shows the tracks at Appomattox Station where three supply trains containing provisions for the Confederate army were overtaken and captured by Custer's cavalry on April 8. The photographer stands on the right-hand track. (Library of Congress LC-DIG-ppmsca-12618)

timber and brush, the area at his front was unsuitable for either artillery or cavalry operations.

Custer's 1st Brigade, commanded by Colonel Alexander Pennington, launched several uncoordinated attacks against Walker's artillerymen but was quickly thrown back by canister fired at close range. His 3rd Brigade, mainly consisting of West Virginians under Colonel Henry Capehart, attacked next and was also repulsed. At about 8 p.m. Custer led his whole division, including Wells's 2nd Brigade, through the woodland and, charging through a hail of canister into what remained of the artillery camp, scattered and captured all those Confederates who had not already retreated. According to one of Sheridan's staff officers, "the hungry gunners … had no stomach for a fight in lieu of a supper, and losing one against their will, had no inclination for the other." During this action Custer's troopers took about 1,000 prisoners, and seized between 25 and 30 cannon, about 200 wagons, and five battle flags. Lee's line of retreat was also blocked. Most of the guns that Walker managed to withdraw were pulled north towards Oakville, although some went west towards Lynchburg or back into Appomattox Court House.

In order to locate the main body of the Confederate army, which had halted in a 4-mile (6.5km) area with fortified breastworks protecting its rear around New Hope Church, Custer sent forward the 15th New York Cavalry, under Lieutenant-Colonel Augustus Root, who was shot dead by Confederate troops as he entered the main street at the Court House with his advanced guard. The appearance of these troops in the village and the noise of battle at Appomattox Station was confirmation for Lee that Grant's army was once again at his front as well as his rear. Establishing his headquarters about a mile from Appomattox Court House, he held what turned out to be his last council of war with Longstreet, Gordon and Fitzhugh Lee, and concluded that if it could be established that only Sheridan's cavalry stood at their front he would attempt a breakthrough towards Lynchburg at dawn. However, it would be another matter if Union infantry had also somehow managed to arrive behind their cavalry, but Lee doubted their capability to march so far that quickly. He chose generals Gordon and "Rooney" Lee to lead the next day's movement. They would form a battle line along the western edge of the village and sweep away the Union cavalry blocking the Stage Road heading west. Once this was achieved, his infantry would protect the road and permit the wagons to continue on. But if Union infantry was discovered in their path, Lee was to be informed immediately so that "a flag of truce should be sent to accede to the only alternative left," which was the surrender of the Army of Northern Virginia.

Having joined up with Meade to cross the Appomattox River at Farmville earlier that day, Grant spent the night of April 8/9 at the home of Joseph Crute at Sheppards on the Richmond–Lynchburg Stage Road

To prevent it falling into the hands of Custer's cavalry, artillerymen of Brigadier-General R. Lindsay Walker's brigade destroy a 20-pound Parrott Rifle gun on the night of April 8. Other men can be seen in the background breaking up the railroad track leading west from Appomattox to Lynchburg. (*Battles & Leaders*)

THE LAST "REBEL YELL" – APPOMATTOX COURT HOUSE, APRIL 9, 1865 (PP. 82–83)

The last Confederate attack of the Civil War in Virginia was made at sunrise on April 9, 1865, with Fitzhugh Lee's cavalry **(1)** venting forth the "Rebel Yell" and charging ahead of Gordon's infantry **(2)** with the remnants of Munford's small Virginia Brigade on the extreme right. With the sun at their backs the Virginians brushed to one side the Union cavalry under Colonel Charles H. Smith **(3)** and galloped on until they reached their objective – the Lynchburg Road. Behind them the infantry, with Wallace's South Carolina Brigade on their right wing, also swung round onto the road to hopefully secure their escape route. Shortly after this, while attempting to regroup the remains of his brigade for further action, Munford learned that a Confederate courier had been seen waving a flag of truce and that this was the cause of the stillness that had by then descended around Appomattox Court House.

suffering from a migraine headache, while the still ailing Meade slept in an ambulance a few hundred yards away. At about midnight Grant received a second letter from Lee in which he stated that he intended in his previous communication only to ask what terms might be given and did not propose the surrender of his army but was interested in "the restoration of peace." Grant waited until the next morning and then wrote a response stating that he had "no authority to treat on the subject of peace," but went on to state: "The terms upon which peace can be had are well understood. By the South laying down their arms they will hasten that most desirable event, save thousands of human lives, and hundreds of millions of property not yet destroyed."

In the meantime, the Union infantry of Ord and Griffin pushed on, having marched over 30 miles (50km) in 21 hours by nightfall on April 8. Stopping for a few hours at midnight, they were ordered on to Appomattox Station after only a short rest. Their commanders knew that if Sheridan's cavalry could hold Lee's army up long enough, the infantry might arrive in time to fight a last battle and help end the war, at least in Virginia. Of this experience an officer in the 31st United States Colored Troops recorded: "Most of the march was forced and most trying to the men, who behaved with commendable steadiness and endurance in spite of fatigue and short rations."

Appomattox Court House, April 9

Prior to dawn on Palm Sunday, April 9, Sheridan deployed Smith's 3rd Brigade of Crook's cavalry division to form a dismounted battle line straddling the Stage Road west of Appomattox Court House. Devin's 1st Division was deployed to the right of Smith and south of the Stage Road. As the Confederate line of battle formed, a certain amount of dissent existed among its commanders as generals Gordon and Fitzhugh Lee argued as to whether the infantry or cavalry should lead the advance. Impatient for action, Major-General Bryan Grimes, a divisional commander in Gordon's II Corps, offered to lead off given the command of the other troops. At some point during the morning, Lee sent a dispatch to Gordon enquiring if he believed he could break through the enemy line, to which he replied: "I have fought my corps to a frazzle, and I fear I can do nothing unless I am heavily supported by Longstreet's corps." The Confederate battle line eventually moved forward raising a final "Rebel Yell," with Fitzhugh Lee's cavalry, amounting to about

During the night of April 8/9, Lee held his last council of war with Longstreet, Gordon and Fitzhugh Lee, and decided to attempt a breakthrough at dawn provided only Sheridan's cavalry stood in his way. (Courtesy of the Appomattox Court House National Historical Park)

4,000 troopers, riding ahead of approximately 5,000 infantrymen. Sweeping in on Smith's small brigade, the Confederate troopers captured Union artillery and nearby pickets, and continued to press on towards the main line of troopers, who did their best to give the impression that there was more than just a single brigade of cavalry in the way, and held their ground as long as they could with their mixture of Spencer, Sharps, and Hall carbines, plus rifles. As they inevitably fell back, Crook

sent forward Mackenzie's brigade-sized cavalry division (XXV Corps) and the 2nd Brigade of his own division commanded (following Gregg's capture) by Colonel Samuel Young. Arriving in the fight first, Mackenzie deployed his troopers in line of battle on the high ground behind Smith's former position.

Seeing the Union cavalry falling back, Fitzhugh Lee sent some of "Rooney" Lee's troopers after them. As Lee's troopers rode forward, they encountered Mackenzie's line and scattered it. They next clashed with elements of Young's brigade; Sergeant John Donaldson, Company L, 4th Pennsylvania Cavalry, captured the standard of the 14th Virginia Cavalry, which was the last Confederate battle flag taken in combat during the campaign. Donaldson received a Medal of Honor for his bravery on this occasion.

As Fitzhugh Lee's cavalry punched its way through Crook's dismounted troopers, the Confederate infantry carried out orders and swung in an arc until it faced south along the Stage Road. Indeed, the battle plan had been so successful up to this point that word was sent to General Lee that the tactic had worked and the escape route to Campbell Court House had been opened. Gordon became so confident about this that most of his infantry were ordered to lie down on their arms and rest. As a result, only Cox's North Carolina Brigade of Grimes's Division was facing west in the direction that Ord's infantry was approaching.

At this crucial moment lead infantry elements of Ord's XXIV and XXV corps, led by Major-General John Gibbon, at last appeared out of the woods to the southwest and formed in line of battle, arriving just in time to prevent a Confederate breakout. Behind them the cavalry of Custer, plus Griffin's V Corps, approached the battlefield. Devin's division withdrew from the right of Smith's faltering line, while Custer rode past his rear and fell in behind Griffin's troops. Seeing the massed Union infantry approaching, Devin then withdrew his cavalry and followed Custer.

As Osborn's 1st Brigade of Foster's 1st Division (XXIV Corps) came into view of Cox's Brigade, it immediately charged but was repulsed. Dandy's 3rd Brigade attacked next and was also thrown back with

The Battle of Appomattox Court House, April 9, 1865.

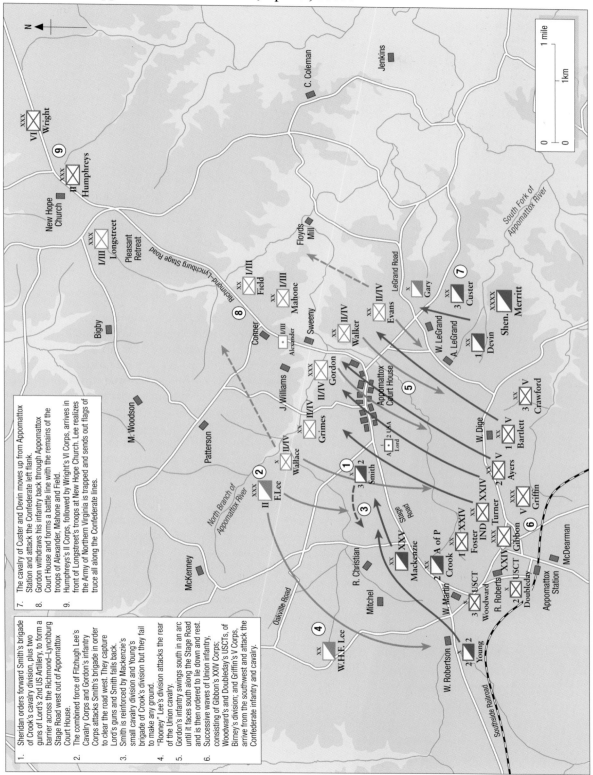

1. Sheridan orders forward Smith's brigade of Crook's cavalry division, plus two guns of Lord's 2nd US Artillery, to form a barrier across the Richmond–Lynchburg Stage Road west out of Appomattox Court House.
2. The combined force of Fitzhugh Lee's Cavalry Corps and Gordon's infantry Corps attacks Smith's brigade in order to clear the road west. They capture Lord's guns and Smith falls back.
3. Smith is reinforced by Mackenzie's small cavalry division and Young's brigade of Crook's division but they fail to make any ground.
4. "Rooney" Lee's division attacks the rear of the Union cavalry.
5. Gordon's infantry swings south in an arc until it faces south along the Stage Road and is then ordered to lie down and rest.
6. Successive waves of Union infantry, consisting of Gibbon's XXIV Corps; Woodward's and Doubleday's USCTs, of Birney's division; and Griffin's V Corps, arrive from the southwest and attack the Confederate infantry and cavalry.
7. The cavalry of Custer and Devin moves up from Appomattox Station and attack the Confederate left flank.
8. Gordon withdraws his infantry back through Appomattox Court House and forms a battle line with the remains of the troops of Alexander, Mahone and Field.
9. Humphreys's II Corps, followed by Wright's VI Corps, arrives in front of Longstreet's troops at New Hope Church. Lee realizes the Army of Northern Virginia is trapped and sends out flags of truce all along the Confederate lines.

87

the 11th Maine being temporarily cut off by Confederate cavalry. Foster's remaining brigade, commanded by Colonel Harrison Fairchild, joined the rest of the division, which by then had sought refuge in a ravine to await further reinforcements. The next troops to arrive were those of Turner's Independent infantry plus Woodward's (3rd) and Doubleday's (2nd) brigades of US Colored Troops, of Birney's 2nd Division, temporarily attached to XXIV Corps. Observing their approach, an orderly rode by the beleaguered Union cavalry shouting, "Keep up your courage, boys; the infantry is coming right along – in two columns – black and white – side by side – a regular checker-board." By this time the Confederate infantry began to realize their path was blocked by massed Union infantry in support of cavalry and prepared to face the inevitable.

Becoming aware of the seriousness of the situation, the cavalry under Rosser and Munford rode off towards Lynchburg rather than face surrender. As Griffin's V Corps arrived south of the village adding to the massed infantry at his front, and with the cavalry of Custer and Devin on their right, Gordon withdrew the remainder of his infantry back through Appomattox Court House and into Appomattox River Valley, beyond where a last, desperate battle line was formed by General E.P. Alexander which also consisted of the remains of the divisions of Mahone and Wilcox.

In the Confederate rear at New Hope Church, Humphreys's II Corps arrived in front of Longstreet's entrenched rearguard which consisted of Field's Division, with Wright's VI Corps also approaching rapidly behind. Faced with Ord's Army of the James to the west, Griffin's V Corps and Sheridan's cavalry on his southwestern flank, and two army corps to the northeast, the only avenue of escape left open to Lee was to the northwest, which was devoid of major highways and blocked by a bridgeless James River. He was left with no alternative but to meet with Grant to discuss terms for the surrender of the Army of Northern Virginia.

AFTERMATH

Word of a ceasefire spread through the Confederate ranks as couriers carrying white truce flags rode or ran up and down the battle lines, but further casualties occurred before the firing finally stopped at about 11 a.m. Advancing in the skirmish line formed by the 155th Pennsylvania, 19-year-old Private William Montgomery was mortally wounded by an exploding artillery round and died 19 days later. Struck down by further artillery fire landing in front of Chamberlain's 1st Brigade (1st Division, V Corps), 1st Lieutenant Hiram Clark, 185th New York, was the last Federal officer to be killed at Appomattox. Altogether, a total of about 2,000 men from both armies were killed, wounded or captured in the last two battles.

With the passage of truce flags through Union lines, general officers such as Ord, Gibbon and Griffin rode out towards the Court House, where they met with the likes of Longstreet, Gordon and Heth. In the meantime, while the truce flag remained to be shown, hostilities threatened to continue. Facing Sheridan's two divisions along the LeGrand Road, Gary's cavalry supported by artillery and engineers serving as infantry were still forming a line of battle in preparation to meet a charge from Custer's cavalry when the word finally reached them. Brigade Bugler Nathaniel Sisson recalled: "We advanced and met the enemy's skirmish line, brushing them before us easily. In a short time we were advancing, apparently, on Lee's wagon train, but, instead, we soon found ourselves headed through Lee's army. Then the last bugle command of a hostile nature was blown and we were charging at them. As we rushed on two of General Gordon's aids [sic] rode out carrying a flag of truce. That practically ended the war." Approached by one of the truce flag bearers after ordering a halt, Custer remarked: "We will listen to no terms but that of unconditional surrender. We are behind your army now and it is at our mercy."

Entitled "The Surrender," this painting by Keith Rocco shows an accurate representation of those present in the parlor of the McLean house on April 9. The only other Confederate officer there during the 90-minute meeting between Lee and Grant was Lieutenant-Colonel Charles Marshall. Apart from Grant, the other 13 Union officers included Major-General Edward O. C. Ord, standing with arms folded at center, Major-General Philip H. Sheridan, seated fourth from right, and the President's son, Captain Robert Todd Lincoln, who stands with hand on chair. (Courtesy of Appomattox Court House National Historical Park)

Earlier that morning, Lee had ridden north to New Hope Church in hope of meeting Grant as soon as possible, expecting the Union commander to approach from that direction. However, Grant was still on his way to join Sheridan and Ord. Instead Lee was handed Grant's note containing a reply that proposed terms for the restoration of peace, but required the Confederate forces to lay down their arms and surrender. In order to arrange a meeting, Lee sent two messages through the lines hoping one or the other would reach the Union commander quickly. One was passed through Humphreys's skirmish line at New Hope Church while a duplicate was conveyed by way of Sheridan's front to the south of the Court House. Both stated: "I received your note of this morning on the picket-line, whither I had come to meet you and ascertain definitely what terms were embraced in your proposal of yesterday with reference to the surrender of this army. I now ask an interview in accordance with the offer contained in your letter of yesterday for that purpose."

Still suffering from a migraine, Grant received the first copy of Lee's third letter at about 11.50 a.m. while he was still about 5 miles (8km) away from Appomattox Court House having passed through Walker's Church with his entourage. The Union commander later recalled: "When the officer reached me I was still suffering from the sick-headache; but the instant I saw the contents of the note I was cured." When General John A. Rawlins read the message aloud, the officers gathering around greeted the news with a subdued three cheers followed by tears of relief from some. At last it seemed that the war was over, at least in Virginia. Grant dismounted and penned a reply in which he explained that he would push on and meet Lee, which was delivered by Union staff officer Colonel Orville E. Babcock.

Meanwhile, the Confederate commander and his aide-de-camp Lieutenant-Colonel Charles Marshall, plus an orderly, looked for somewhere suitable to hold a surrender conference in Appomattox Court House; they encountered Wilmer McLean, who offered the use of his home on the western edge of the community. McLean had actually moved to Appomattox from Manassas during the fall of 1862 to avoid further exposure to battle after experiencing the events of 1861–62. Lee entered and sat in McLean's parlor to await the arrival of Grant. The Union commander arrived about 1 p.m. and was accompanied by 12 other officers including Sheridan and Ord. Meade, Humphreys and Wright were still 4 miles (6.5km) away in Lee's rear.

After some initial small talk about their earlier military service together in the Mexican War, Lee cut the conversation short stating: "General, I have come to … treat about the surrender of my army, and I think the best way would be for you to put your terms in writing." Grant responded by setting out the following terms in a manifold order-book which provided three copies, stipulating: "Rolls of all the officers and men to be made in duplicate … officers to give their individual paroles not to take up arms against the Government of the United States until properly exchanged … The arms, artillery, and public property are to be parked and stacked, and turned over to the officers appointed … to receive them. This will not embrace the side-arms of the officers, nor their private horses or baggage. This done, officers and men will be allowed to return to his home, not to be disturbed by the U.S. authority so long as they observe their paroles and the laws in force where they may reside." Lee responded by pointing out that his cavalrymen and artillerymen owned their own horses, having brought them into service in exchange for 40 cents a day received as part of their monthly pay. Realizing that much of Lee's army were probably farmers who would need their animals for the spring planting, Grant promised to instruct his officers to allow them to keep their mounts upon departure for home. Lee then responded in writing agreeing to the terms, and the deed was done.

Grant wore a plain officer's sack coat for his fateful meeting with Lee at Appomattox Court House on April 9. In his memoirs he recalled: "When I had left camp that morning I had not expected so soon the result that was then taking place, and consequently was in rough garb. I was without a sword, as I usually was when on horseback on the field, and wore a soldier's blouse for a coat, with the shoulder straps of my rank to indicate to the army who I was." (Courtesy of the Texas Civil War Museum)

Before the two generals parted company, the subject of rations was raised and Grant enquired how many men were still in Lee's army. Due to the heavy casualties sustained, plus numerous stragglers and some deserters, Lee could not tell him. However, Grant offered 25,000 rations supplied from those designated for XXIV Corps. Before he left for his headquarters, Grant also appointed generals Gibbon, Griffin and Merritt to serve as commissioners to arrange details of the surrender. Later that day Lee appointed Longstreet, Gordon and Pendleton for the same purpose.

With negotiations completed, Lee returned to his shattered army to bid it farewell. Lee met Grant again in the chilly drizzling rain on the morning of April 10. Grant tried to persuade Lee to surrender the three remaining Confederate armies, as he had only surrendered the Army of Northern Virginia, but Lee declined. As a result, other Confederate field armies would continue to operate throughout the South for the next two months, but no large battles were fought. The formal surrender parade took place at Appomattox Court House two days later. Starting at 6 a.m. it was not finished until 1 p.m. The records indicate that 27,950 officers and men of Lee's army were given their paroles between April 10 and April 12. A total of 6,226 Confederate soldiers were killed and wounded during the campaign while the Federals sustained 8,628 killed and wounded. Once the ceremony was finished and all their arms were stacked, the former Confederate soldiers were free to begin their journey home as civilians.

Seventy-two Confederate flags were surrendered at Appomattox Court House on April 12, while many others were smuggled home, destroyed or cut up by the men who had carried them into battle. The wool bunting and cotton battle flag of the 61st Virginia Infantry was taken home by a Connecticut soldier and years later presented to the US National Park Service by the widow of Civil War historian Douglas Southall Freeman, whose father Walker Buford Freeman had served with the regiment during the war. (Courtesy of the Appomattox Court House National Park)

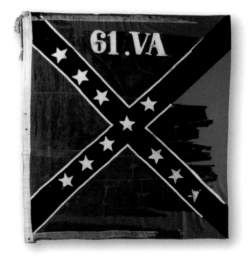

THE BATTLEFIELD TODAY

A visit to the Appomattox Campaign battle sites should begin in the Petersburg area. Using the Virginia Trail map, motorists can follow Lee's Retreat Driving Tour, which traces the route of the Army of Northern Virginia from Petersburg to Appomattox Court House. Short-range radio messages at these markers provide battle details and descriptions when the radio is tuned to AM 1610. Also along the trail are numerous Virginia Historical Highway Markers.

At Appomattox Plantation in Hopewell, about 6 miles (10km) northeast of Petersburg, is Grant's Cabin, which served as his headquarters until the end of the siege operations. The Petersburg National Battlefield, operated by the National Park Service (NPS), consists of a 4-mile (6km) drive included within which are four short interpretative walking trails. The Eastern Front Visitor Center, or Blue Tour Stop 1, contains a three-dimensional map presentation of the military operations during the Petersburg Campaign, plus museum exhibits. The grass-covered earthworks of Fort Stedman are found at Blue Tour Stop 5, plus a loop trail which leads to Colquitt's Salient where originated the Confederate attack of March 25, 1865. At Blue Tour Stop 6 are the remains of Fort Haskell, the guns of which helped Union forces retake Fort Stedman on the above date.

Located southwest of Petersburg along the Boydton Plank Road, the Pamplin Park Civil War Site commemorates the Union VI Corps breakthrough on April 2 and consists of four museums, including the National Museum of the Civil War Soldier, and four antebellum homes, plus living history venues. An extended driving tour of about 16 miles (26km) leads to battlefield park areas farther south and west of Petersburg. Open seasonally, the NPS Western Front Visitor Contact Station is just east of the Vaughan Road and at Red Tour Stop 2 can be found the Poplar Grove cemetery; the latter contains the remains of 6,314 Confederate and Union soldiers who died in the Petersburg and Appomattox campaigns. About two-thirds of these graves are marked "unknown." The remains of another 5,000 Union soldiers who died of wounds or disease in the hospitals at City Point were buried in makeshift cemeteries nearby. These were later reinterred in the City Point National Cemetery in Hopewell. Many more of the Confederate soldiers who died during the campaign and siege were buried in mass graves at Blandford Cemetery in Petersburg.

During their April 10 meeting, Grant and Lee agreed each surrendered Confederate soldier would be provided with an individual "Paroled Prisoner's Pass," which would aid their journey home, allowing them to use federal transportation where available or to draw food and supplies from federally controlled stations in the South. Approximately 30,000 blank passes were printed at the Clover Hill Tavern. The example shown is that issued to Major-General Fitzhugh Lee. (Courtesy of Appomattox Court House National Historical Park)

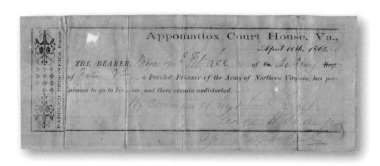

The grass-covered earthwork remains of Fort Gregg can be seen near Red Tour Stop 4, while the Ambrose P. Hill death-site marker is located about 1 mile (1.6km) west on the right of the Boydton Plank Road. Another historical marker stands on the White Oak Road at the site of the Union assault of March 31. Five more NPS Green Tour Stop markers surround the Five Forks Battlefield Visitor Contact Station. Stop 1 indicates the starting point for the attack on the Confederate trenches at the White Oak Road by Merritt's dismounted cavalry. The angle, or "return," at the eastern end of the White Oak Road Confederate defenses is found at Stop 2, while the Five Forks Intersection is located at Stop 3. The Final Stand made by "Rooney" Lee's cavalry is at Stop 4, and Stop 5 denotes the point where Crawford's 3rd Division emerged on Ford's Road and struck the rear of the Confederate line.

Much of the battlefield in the vicinity of Amelia Court House, including Paineville and Jetersville, is heavily wooded, privately owned and difficult to interpret. A Lee's Retreat marker in Jetersville commemorates the battle involving African-American Confederate troops at Paineville, while other markers are found at Jetersville, Amelia Springs and Deatonsville. A further marker is located at Holt's Corner approaching the Little Sailor's Creek battlefield.

At the Sailor's Creek Battlefield Historical State Park can be found a visitor's center that contains a museum and research library, Battlefield Memorial and the Overton/Hillsman Farmhouse which is restored as a field hospital with bloodstains still visible on the original wooden floor where the surgeons' operating table stood. The battlefield also has at least eight other Lee's Retreat markers, linked by two walking trails, including those devoted to "Crossing Little Sailor's Creek," "Assaulting the Confederate Battle Line," "Ewell's Line of Defense," and "Victory or Death." The "Confederate Overlook Trail" guides visitors to the creek itself.

Open by appointment only, the small, privately owned High Bridge Civil War Museum displays a

LEFT
Given the task of receiving the official surrender of the Confederate infantry on April 12, the 155th Pennsylvania stand at right. (Painting by Kenneth Riley, 1961, courtesy of West Point Museum Collection, US Military Academy)

RIGHT
A Confederate soldier returns to his shattered home to rebuild his life at the end of the Civil War. (West Point Museum Collection, US Military Academy)

BELOW
Civilians are shown celebrating Lee's surrender of April 9. The euphoria was short-lived, with the assassination of Lincoln five days later, and it was not until August 20, 1865 that President Andrew Johnson formally declared the Civil War at an end. (West Point Museum Collection, US Military Academy)

collection of artifacts and is situated on the High Bridge battlefield. A Virginia Historic Landmark, the High Bridge railroad trestle stands in High Bridge Trail State Park and is part of a 31-mile (50km)-long trail. Further markers are found at Farmville, Cumberland Church and New Store. The final two battlefields are part of the Appomattox Court House National Historical Park and include a Visitor Center at Appomattox Court House, where a Wall of Honor rotating display can be viewed; the McLean House, site of the final surrender; the Clover Hill Tavern, which contains the Parole Pass exhibit; and various other period buildings. Other aspects of the battlefield such as the New Hope Church trenches can be explored using the Cell Phone Tour. The Museum of the Confederacy – Appomattox is situated just west of the Park on Horseshoe Road.

SELECT BIBLIOGRAPHY

A Biographical History of Nordaway and Atchison Counties, Missouri (Chicago, Illinois: The Lewis Publishing Company, 1901)

Arnold, William B., *The Fourth Massachusetts Cavalry in the Closing Scenes of the War for the Maintenance of the Union – From Richmond to Appomattox* (Boston: publisher unknown)

Atlas to Accompany the Official Records of the Union and Confederate Armies (Washington DC: Government Printing Office, 1891–95)

Calkins, Chris M., *Thirty-six Hours before Appomattox* (Farmville, Virginia: The Farmville Herald, 1980)

——, *The Final Bivouac: The Surrender Parade at Appomattox and the Disbanding of the Armies – April 10 – May 20, 1865* (Lynchburg, Virginia: H.E. Howard, Inc., 1988)

——, *The Appomattox Campaign, March 29 – April 9, 1865* (Lynchburg, Virginia: Schroeder Publications, 2008)

Chamberlain, Brevet Major-General Joshua L., "The Military Operations on the White Oak Road, Virginia, March 31, 1865," *War Papers read before the State of Maine Commandery of the Military Order of the Loyal Legion of the United States*, Vol. 1 (Portland, Maine: The Thurston Print and Lefavor-Tower Company, 1898)

Confederate Veteran Magazine, 32 vols (Nashville, Tennessee: Trustees of the Confederate Veterans, 1893–1932)

Driver, Robert J. (Jr.), *1st Virginia Cavalry* (Lynchburg, Virginia: H.H. Howard, Inc., 1991)

Fox, John J., III, *The Confederate Alamo: Bloodbath at Petersburg's Fort Gregg on April 2, 1865* (Winchester, Virginia: Angle Valley Press, 2010)

Freeman, Douglas S., *Lee's Lieutenants: A Study in Command*, Vol. 3 (New York: Scribner, 1946)

Hewett, Janet B., *Supplement to the Official Records of the Union and Confederate Armies*, 100 vols (Wilmington, NC: Broadfoot Publishing Co., 1994–2001)

Krick, Robert K., *Civil War Weather in Virginia* (Tuscaloosa, Alabama: University of Alabama Press, 2007)

Lee, Captain Robert E., *Recollections and Letters of General Robert E. Lee* (Westminster, England: Archibald, Constable & Co., Ltd, 1904)

Longacre, Edward G., *The Cavalry at Appomattox: A Tactical Study of Mounted Operations During the Civil War's Climatic Campaign, March 27–April 9, 1865* (Mechanicsburg, Pennsylvania: Stackpole Books, 2003)

Longstreet, Helen D., *Lee and Longstreet at High Tide* (Gainesville, Georgia: privately published, 1905)

Manarin, Louis H. (ed.), *Richmond at War: Minutes of the City Council 1861–1865* (Chapel Hill, North Carolina: University of North Carolina Press, 1966)

Marvel, William, *Lee's Last Retreat: The Flight to Appomattox* (Chapel Hill, North Carolina: University of North Carolina Press: 2002)

Maxfield, Albert, *The Story of One Regiment: The 11th Maine Infantry Volunteers in the War of the Rebellion* (New York: J.J. Little, 1896)

Newhall, Colonel Frederick C., *With General Sheridan in Lee's Last Campaign* (Philadelphia, Pennsylvania: J.P. Lippencott & Co., 1866)

Personal Memoirs of Ulysses S. Grant, Vol. II (New York: Charles L. Webster & Company, 1886)

Pickett, LaSalle Corbell, *Pickett and His Men* (Atlanta, Georgia: Foote & Davies, 1899)

Scott, Robert N., *Official Records of the War of the Rebellion*, 127 vols (Washington DC: Government Printing Office, 1880–1901)

Southern Historical Society Papers, 52 vols. (1876–1959) (New York: Millswood, 1979)

Tobie, Edward Parsons, *History of the First Maine Cavalry, 1861–65* (Boston, Massachusetts: Press of Emory & Hughs, 1887)

Wilson Greene, A., *Civil War Petersburg: Confederate City in the Crucible of War* (Charlottesville, Virginia: University Press of Virginia, 2006)

Various newspapers

INDEX

African-American troops **56–57, 59, 60, 61**; *see also* Army of the James: XXV Corps
Alexander, Brigadier-General Edward Porter 76, **86, 88**
Amelia Court House **4**, 36, 44, **46**, 54–55, 60
Anderson, Richard H.
  background 13, 14
  and Confederate withdrawal 74
  and fall of Petersburg and Richmond 25–26, 26–34
  and Little Sailor's Creek 65–69
  relieved of command 78
  and White Oak Road 28, 30
Appomattox Court House **89**
Appomattox Court House, Battle of (1865) **4, 82–83**, 85–88, **86, 87**, 94
Appomattox River **4**, 44–47, **44, 45**, 54, 55, 62–65, 73, 74–76
Appomattox Station, Battle of (1865) **4**, 78–81, **79, 80**, 94
Army of Northern Virginia
  I Corps 13, 26–34, 40, 43, 45–47, 61
  II Corps 13–14, **14, 22**, 23, 30, 34, 42, 44–45, 85
  III Corps 14, 26, 34, 36, 40, 45, 61
  IV Corps 14, 25, 28, 30, 49–54
  Anderson's Corps 13, 14, 28, 52, 65–69, 73, 78
  battle order 19–21
  before Appomattox 6, 9–11
  Cavalry Corps 14
  commanders 9–11
  overview 13–15
  prisoners 33
  surrender 75, 77, 78, 81–85, 88–91, **90, 93**
  Tucker's Naval Brigade 45, 68, **70–71**
Army of the James
  XXIV Corps 14–15, **15**, 22, 38–39, 41, 49, 60, 63, 86–88
  XXV Corps 14, 15, 22, 24, 30, 31, 42, 48, 86
  battle order 18–19
  before Appomattox 5
  and fall of Petersburg and Richmond 22, 24
  and forts Gregg and Whitworth 38–39, 41, 42, 43
  overview 14–15
  and pursuit of Confederates 60–65, 76, 80, 85–86, 86–88
Army of the Potomac
  II Corps 14, 23, 24, 25. 27, 29, 35, 43, 46, 49, 54, 60–65, 66–67, 73, 74–76, 78, 87, 88
  V Corps 14, 23, 24, 25–26, 27, 28–33, **30**, 42, 46, 49, 55–59, 60–65, 74, 80, 87
  VI Corps 14, 34–35, 37, 38–39, 42, 43, 46, 47–48, 49, 54, 60–65, 68–69, 73, 74, 75, 76, 78, 87, 88
  IX Corps 14, 22, 34, 42, 43, 47, 49, 54
  battle order 15–18
  before Appomattox 5
  commanders 11–12
  overview 14
Army of the Shenandoah
  battle order 17–18
  before Appomattox 5
  commanders 12
  and fall of Petersburg and Richmond 23, 24–25, 27
  overview 14, 15

and pursuit of Confederates 30–33, **30**, 42, 49–54, 66–67, **70–71**
Army of the Tennessee 5–6, 26

Barringer, Brigadier-General Rufus 50, 51, 52–53, **54**
Barton, Seth 69
Biri (Bery/Berry), Laurent 41
Boydton Plank Road **4**, 23, 24, 25–26, **25, 26**, 27, 34–35
Breckinridge, John C. 6, 23, 26, 36, 74, 78
Briscoe, Colonel James C. 37
bugles **88**
Burgess Mill 26, 34
Burkeville Junction 23, 48, 60
Burnside, Ambrose 14

cemeteries 92
Chamberlain, Brigadier-General Joshua L. 25, **28, 29**
City Point 5, 6, 7
Clark, Hiram **86, 88, 89**
clothing and uniforms **15**, 79, **86, 91**
Colston, Lieutenant Frederick 59, 60
Confederate forces
  strategy and plans 23
  see also Army of Northern Virginia; Army of the Tennessee
Corse, Montgomery 69
Crawford, Brigadier-General Samuel W. 27, 28, 31, 32–33
Crook, Major-General George
  and Appomattox Court House 85–86
  and Appomattox Station 79–80
  and Cumberland Church 74, 77
  and Little Sailor's Creek 66–67, 69
  and pursuit of Confederates 54, 55, 59, 62
Crow House redoubt 35, 43
Cumberland Church, Battle of (1865) **4**, 74–78, **75, 94**
Cunningham, Private Richard **64**
Custer, Brigadier-General George C. **51**
  and Appomattox Court House 86, 87
  and Appomattox Station 79, 81
  and Confederate surrender 89
  and Dinwiddie Court House 27–28
  and Five Forks 33
  and Little Sailor's Creek 65, 66–67, 69
  and Namozine Church 49–54
  and pursuit of Confederates 74

Davies, Brigadier-General Henry E. 27, 58, 59–60, 77
Davis, Jefferson 36, 44, 73
Dimmock's Line 34, 35, **43**
Dinwiddie Court House **4**, 24–25, **25**, 26–28, **26**
Donaldson, Sergeant John 86
DuBose, Dudley 69
Duncan, Captain James H. 40

Early, Jubal 13–14
Ewell, Lieutenant-General Richard S.
  command 13
  and Confederate withdrawal 45, 46, 47, 55, 61
  and fall of Petersburg and Richmond 34
  and Little Sailor's Creek 66–67, 68–69

Five Forks **4**, 26–27, **26**, 29–34, **31, 32, 33**, 93
flags **91**
Fort Mahone 34, 42, **43**
Fort Owen 37
Fort Stedman, attack on (1865) **4, 22**, 23, 92
Forts Gregg and Whitworth 35, 36–44, **37, 38–39**, 93
Freeman, Douglas Southell 10, 91

Gary, Brigadier-General Martin W. 47, 59, 79, 80, 87, 89
Gaul, Gilbert, paintings by **68**
Gibbon, Major-General John
  command 14
  and Confederate surrender 89, 91
  and fall of Petersburg and Richmond 24
  and forts Gregg and Whitworth 38–39, 41
  and pursuit of Confederates 60, 86
Goddard, Captain John D.B. 64
Gordon, Major-General John B. **10, 85**
  at Appomattox Court House 81, 84, 85, 86, 87, 88
  background and character 10
  and Confederate surrender 81, 89
  and Confederate withdrawal 42, 73, 74, 77–78
  and Cumberland Church 76
  at Fort Stedman 22, 23
  and Little Sailor's Creek 69
Grant, Lieutenant-General Ulysses S. **6, 11, 90**
  background and character 5, 11
  and Confederate surrender 75, 77, 78. 81–85, 88, 90–91
  and fall of Petersburg and Richmond 26, 29, 31, 33
  jacket worn by **91**
  on Meade 12
  and pursuit of Confederates 48–49, 60, 73
  strategy and plans 7, 22–23
Gregg, General J. Irvin 77
Griffin, Brigadier-General Charles
  and Appomattox Court House 85, 86, 88
  command 14
  and Confederate surrender 89, 91
  and fall of Petersburg and Richmond 27, 28, 29, 31, 33, 42
  and pursuit of Confederates 54, 74, 80

Hamblin, Colonel Joseph E. 37, 38–39
Hampton, Lieutenant-General Wade 11, 14, 26
Hatcher's Run 26, 34, 36, 42
Healy, G.P.A.: paintings by **6**
High Bridge **4**, 60–65, **62, 63**, 73, 74–76, 93–94
Hill, Lieutenant-General Ambrose P. **10–11, 10**, 14, 35, 93
Hillsman Farmhouse **4**, 65, **66–67**, 68, **68**, **74**, 93
Hodges, Captain William T. 64
Holt's Corner **66–67**, 93
Humphreys, Major-General Andrew A.
  and Appomattox Court House 87, 88
  and Appomattox Station 78
  command 14
  and Confederate surrender 90
  and Cumberland Church 75, 76
  and fall of Petersburg and Richmond 23, 25, 26, 27, 29, 35, 43

and Little Sailor's Creek 66–67, 69, 73, 74
and pursuit of Confederates 54, 60, 62
Hunton, Eppa 69

Janeway, Colonel Hugh 58, 59
Jetersville, Battle of (1865) 55–58, 93
Johnson, Major-General Bushrod **50**
    and fall of Petersburg and Richmond 25–26,
        28–29, 42–44
    and Namozine Church 49–50, 51, 52–53
    relieved of command 78
Johnston, Lieutenant-General Joseph 6, 26, 27

Kershaw, Major-General Joseph B. 34, 45–47,
    55, 61, 66–67, 68, 69

Lee, Major-General Fitzhugh **10**, 85
    and Appomattox Court House 84, 85, 86, 87
    background and character 11, 14
    and Confederate surrender 81
    and Confederate withdrawal 55, 78
    and fall of Petersburg and Richmond 26,
        27, 42–44
    and Namozine Church 49, 50, 51, 52–53
    and Paineville 58, 59, 60
    parole pass **92**
Lee, George Washington Custis 45, 47,
    55, 68
Lee, General Robert E. **8**, 85, **90**
    and Appomattox Court House 85, 86
    background and character 9
    and Confederate withdrawal 44, 45, 47, 54,
        55–59, 61–62, 63, 65, 73, 74, 78
    and Cumberland Church 75, 76, 77
    and fall of Petersburg and Richmond 24, 26,
        28, 29, 30, 34, 35, 42
    strategy and plans 6, 7, 23
    surrenders 75, 77, 78, 81, 85, 88, 90–91
Lee, Major-General William Henry Fitzhugh
        "Rooney"
    and Appomattox Court House 81, 86, 87
    and Confederate withdrawal 61
    and fall of Petersburg and Richmond 4, 27,
        30, 33, 42–44
    and Little Sailor's Creek 66–67, 69
    and Namozine Church 50, 51, 52–53
    and Plaineville 59
Lincoln, Abraham 6, 7, 9, 11, 48, 73, 93
Lincoln, Captain Robert Todd 90
Little Sailor's Creek, Battles of (1865) **4**, 65–74,
    66–67, 68, 70–71, 73, 74, 93
Longstreet, Major-General James **10, 85**
    background and character 9–10, 13, 14
    and Confederate surrender 74, 77, 81, 89
    and Confederate withdrawal 40, 45, 47, 54,
        61, 63, 73, 77, 78
    Lee summons 34, 35, 36

McElroy, 1st Lieutenant Frank 36, 37,
    38–39, 40
McGowan, Brigadier-General Samuel 26, 28,
    35–36
MacKenzie, Brigadier-General Ranald S. 22, 30,
    31, 86, 87
McLean, Wilmer 89, 90
Mahone, Major-General William
    and Appomattox Court House 87
    and Confederate withdrawal 45, 55, 61
    and Cumberland Church 74–77
    and forts Gregg and Whitworth 38–39,
        40
    and Little Sailor's Creek 66–67

Marshall, Lieutenant-Colonel Charles 90, **90**
Marshall's Crossroads **4**, 65, **66–67**
Meade, Major-General George G. **12**
    background and character 11–12
    and Confederate surrender 90
    and fall of Petersburg and Richmond 29, 42
    and pursuit of Confederates 48, 59, 60,
        81–85
Merritt, Major-General Wesley
    and Appomattox Court House 87
    and Appomattox Station 80
    and Confederate surrender 91
    and Five Forks 30
    and Little Sailor's Creek 66–67, 68, 69
    and pursuit of Confederates 54
Munford, Brigadier-General Thomas T.
    and Appomattox Court House 84
    and Confederate withdrawal 27
    and Cumberland Church 76, 77
    and Five Forks 30
    and High Bridge 63, 64
    surrender avoided by 88

Namozine Church, Battle of (1865) **4,** 49–54,
    52–53
Newhall, Captain Frederick C. 24, 26

Ord, Major-General Edward O.C. **90**
    and Appomattox Court House 85, 86
    and Appomattox Station 80
    command 14
    and Confederate surrender 89, 90
    and High Bridge 60–65
    and pursuit of Confederates 42
O'Sullivan, Timothy: photos by **44, 62,
    63, 80**
Owen, Lieutenant-Colonel William Miller 37,
    38–39

Paineville, Battle of (1865) **56–57,** 59–60, **60,
    61,** 93
Pamplin Park Civil War Site 92
Parke, Major-General John G.
    command 14
    and fall of Petersburg and Richmond 22,
        34, 42, 43
    and pursuit of Confederates 49, 54, 59
parole passes **92**
Petersburg, siege of (1864–65) 5, 6–7, 9, 22–23
    Confederate withdrawal 44–47
    fall 24–44, **43**
    National Battlefield 92
    Union occupation 47–48, **47, 48**
Philippoteaux, Paul Dominique: paintings by **32**
Pickett, Major-General George E. **29**
    and fall of Petersburg and Richmond 26–33,
        42–44
    and Little Sailor's Creek 65, 66–67, 68, 69
    and pursuit of Confederates 51, 61
    relieved of command 78
Pilcher, Private W.S. **78, 79**
Porter, Rear Admiral David D. 6, 7

Read, Brigadier-General Theodore 63
Richmond
    Confederate withdrawal 44–47
    fall 24–44, **49**
    siege of (1864–65) 5, 6–7, 10, 22–23
    Union occupation 48
Richmond & Danville Railroad 24, 26, 36, 54
River Queen (dispatch steamer) 6, 7
Root, Lieutenant-Colonel Augustus 81

Rosser, Major-General Thomas L.
    and Cumberland Church 76
    and fall of Petersburg and Richmond 27,
        29, 30
    and High Bridge 63, 64
    and Namozine Church 50, 52–53
    surrender avoided by 88

St. John, Isaac M. 54, 62, 74
Schofield, Major-General John M. 5
Sheppard, W.L.: sketches by **49**
Sheridan, Major-General Philip H. **12, 25, 30,
    90**
    and Appomattox Court House 85, 87
    and Appomattox Station 78–80
    background and character 7, 12
    and Confederate surrender 90
    and fall of Petersburg and Richmond
        24–25, 27
    at Five Forks 30–33
    and Little Sailor's Creek 65, 68, 73
    and Namozine Church 50
    and pursuit of Confederates 48–49, 54, 55,
        59, 60, 63, 74
Sherman, Major-General William T. 5, 6, 7
Sims, James 69
Sims, Captain Robert M. **89**
Sisson, Brigade Bugler Nathaniel **88, 89**
Smith, Colonel Charles H. 65, **82–83,** 85, 87
Southside Railroad **4,** 24, 26, **26,** 34, 35–36,
    49, **63**
Stuart, J.E.B. 10, 12, 14
Stiles, Major Robert 69, 72

Talcott, Colonel Thomas M. 44, 74
Terry, Brigadier-General William R. 30,
    32–33
Trobriand, Brigadier-General Philip Régis de
    62, 69

Union forces **15**
    commanders 11–12
    overview 14–15
    strategy and plans 22–23
    see also Army of the James; Army of the
        Potomac; Army of the Shenandoah

Valley Campaign (1865) 12, 15
Venable, Colonel C.S. 35

Walker, Brigadier-General Reuben L. 38–39,
    40, 80–81
Warren, Major-General Gouverneur K. **32**
    command 14
    and fall of Petersburg and Richmond 23, 24,
        26, 27, 28–29, 30–31
    removal from command 31, 33
Washburn, Colonel Francis 63–65, **65**
Waud, Alfred R.: drawings by **31, 37, 47, 60,
    73, 74, 86, 89**
weapons
    Parrott Rifle guns **81**
    rifle muskets **15**
Weitzel, Major-General Godfrey 15, 22, 48
White Oak Road **4,** 25–26, **26,** 27, 28–29,
    30, 93
Wilcox, Major-General Cadmus 40, 41
Wixsey, Color Sergeant William T. 47
Wright, Major-General Horatio G. 14, 72,
    78, 90

Young, Colonel Samuel 77, 86, 87